Between Worlds

Shared Reflections of a Spiritual Midwife

Between Worlds

Shared Reflections of a Spiritual Midwife

BRÍD SHINE

Bealtaine Press

Between Worlds: Shared Reflections of a Spiritual Midwife

ISBN 978-1-7776535-0-7 (paperback)

These are my memories, from my perspective, and I have tried to represent events as faithfully as possible. Some names and identifying details have been changed to protect the privacy of individuals. This book is not intended as a substitute for direct expert assistance.

Cover photo by Kim Adzich, view from Dzogchen Beara, West Cork, Ireland
Back cover portrait photo by Yvette Monahan, Dublin, Ireland
Book design by Anú Design, Ireland

First published in 2021 by
Bealtaine Press
British Columbia, Canada

www.bridshine.com

Dedicated to the memory of my Mother,
a nurse whose compassionate care of the dying
guided and inspired my life's work

Contents

1

Beginnings

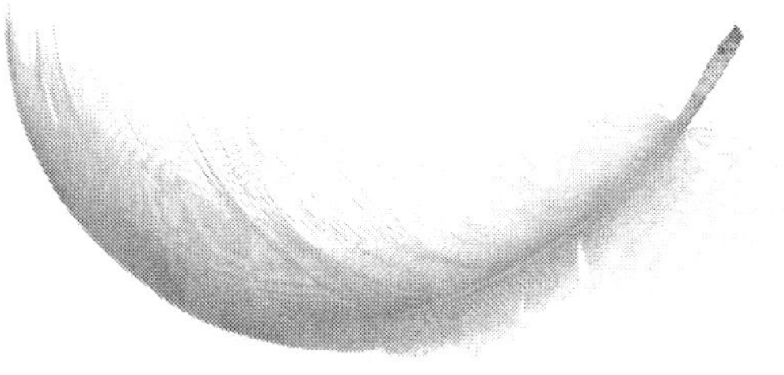

I HAVE BEEN FASCINATED by birth and death my whole life and feel privileged when called upon to be present at either of these transformative events. There is a real sense of otherworldly forces at play on such occasions for it is here that the veil is lifted between the physical and spiritual worlds.

As a nurse and midwife for over thirty years, I have often contemplated life for the baby in the womb during labour and what it must be like when the birthing process comes into full force. I believe our first experience of death is in fact our birth. It ties in with the old saying that death accompanies us our whole life.

The late Irish philosopher John O'Donohue often described this phenomenon.[1] He wrote if you were to talk to a baby in the womb and say to it that life as you know it is about to change, you are going to leave this warm loving environment, be pushed through a dark tunnel and into the light, entering a whole new existence—surely then that baby would feel it was about to die, and be as reluctant about its birth as we are about our death.

---

1 John O'Donohue, *Anam Cara: Spiritual Wisdom from the Celtic World.*

When we come to bury our deceased loved ones, O'Donohue likens this process to that of a caesarean section in reverse; the earth is cut open and we place within it the physical shell of our loved ones, laying them back into the arms of Mother Earth.

In old Celtic times there was a concept known as the spiritual midwife, described by John O'Donohue as someone called upon to preside over births and deaths. Working closely with the fairy realm, she helped birth new souls into the world and helped old souls birth back into the world of spirit. These 'midwives of the dying'[2] used a variety of healing practices including harp music, breath control, poetry and healing oils to soothe the person on the death bed. They were skilled at transforming fear and facilitating peaceful life transitions at the time of physical death. They cared too for the spirit of the deceased, being respectful of the hovering spirit whom we know may have left the physical body but needs time to go towards the drawing force of light into the next life.

This book is composed of stories distilled from my experience of being invited into sacred spaces at the threshold of birth and death. Woven between the individual human stories are my own personal reflections as well as shared wisdom garnered from the different traditions to help us navigate these life events. Within the book are two interviews with my own spiritual midwife and teacher, Maria, an Irish mystic who lives in France and whose wisdom I sought on this journey.

Despite our rich tradition in Ireland of caring for the dying,

2 Richard Groves and Henrietta Anne Klauser, *The American Book of Living and Dying.*

we remain a westernised society where death denial prevails and such events as birth and death have become highly medicalised. It is therefore befitting, in this time of awakening consciousness, that we gather some of the old skills and traditions of our Celtic ancestors around these transitions between worlds.

2

Early Experiences of Death

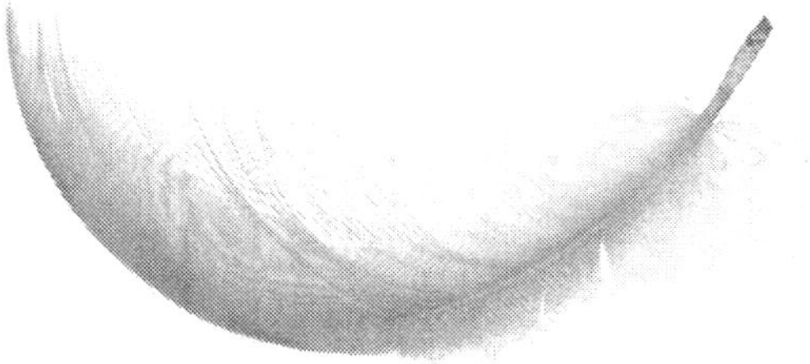

I HAVE BEEN STUDYING death and dying from very early in my childhood, and I am aware that I will remain a student of death until the day I inevitably die myself. My mother was a nurse who frequently tended to the sick and dying of our small rural community in County Kerry, so I grew up understanding death as part of life from a young age. For my own part, since I was old enough to cycle a bike, I became an avid fan of visiting our local graveyard. Most Saturdays, as I would cycle past the back kitchen window of our home, my mother would call out,

'Where are you off to Bríd girl?'

'The graveyard', I would hurl back to her.

There was nothing alarming in my reply. It was in fact met always with approval and oft amusement.

I would go first to my grandfather's grave. He was the only grandparent I had known and I hold his memory to this day with much affection. He died two days after my confirmation when I was twelve years old.

The day before my confirmation my grandfather gave me a big financial gesture: a purple 20 pound note (akin to getting one hundred euro today) and though I tried to be polite by faking protestation at accepting it, in truth my heart knew I would not let it slip through my fingers. He shoved the money into the palm of my hand in front of my mother and told me rather poignantly to please accept it as he would not be around for my next celebration. Letting his sombre tone escape my attention, I curiously asked him what would be my next celebration, to which he answered, 'Your wedding day, Bríd girl'. Two days after that conversation he died of a massive heart attack, much to the distress and grief of us all, in particular my mother.

I also used to visit my uncle Pat at the graveyard. He had lived with us growing up and slept in a small bedroom off our kitchen while his own house was being built. My fondest recollection of him was that he was a great supplier of Cadbury's milk chocolate, divvied out when we, as small children, got rowdy. On the morning of his passing he had asked my mother to call in sick for him to the local hardware store where he was the bookkeeper. I was ten years old and sitting at the kitchen table with my parents when we heard him call out to us in a strange muffled tone. My mother went inquiringly to his bedroom door and all hell broke loose in our home. He'd had a massive heart attack and died that morning despite all efforts to resuscitate him. He was 52 years old.

At his graveside I had a tendency to hang my head a little, because as a child I often felt guilty about his death. My mother had shouted at me that morning to get my neighbour but having seen his bluish face and rigid body from my hovered position at his bedroom door, and feeling my parents' panic, I ran instead to my brother's bedroom where I hid until it was all over. And so it was with a heavy heart that I often told him how sorry I was that I didn't go for help like I had been asked to do the morning he died.

There was a third grave—the grave of a little baby, Séan (pronounced Shane), whom I had grown up beside. He was a beautiful baby boy with white blonde hair and I loved to mind and play with him in my young teenage years. Séan was 18 months old when late one Sunday evening I heard my mother drop the phone in a state of alarm, and I watched as she raced next door to help his family. It was not until I started lectures in my midwifery training and heard the terms 'sunset eyes' and 'bulging fontanel' that I could make sense of his well-known condition of hydrocephalus. I vividly remember minding his two very young siblings the day after he died. There we were in our kitchen making Rice Krispie buns, when the family car carrying the coffin was coming slowly up the road next door. I watched from the safe distance of our small back kitchen window as the little white coffin was carried into their home by his bereft parents. He had been brought home from the hospital where he had died, just a short few days after that phone call to my mother.

So these were the people I visited at the local cemetery, a place where I loved to spend time. It was only a short cycle over our small country road and I enjoyed chatting to the people I knew buried there. I always too, particularly around exams, spent many hours asking them for help. This practice of seeking support from those in spirit started early in my childhood and continues today.

I see and understand death now as merely death in the physical realm. I have been deeply inspired by many spiritual and wisdom teachers who have broadened my understanding of life and death. One teaching I heard by the Vietnamese monk and Buddhist teacher, Thich Nhat Hanh, resonated deeply with me. He talks about 'no birth, no death'[3] and as a philosophy of life, this inspires me. Author Elizabeth Lesser quotes Thich Nhat Hanh saying, 'Our birth certificates are misleading: why, he asks, would a birth certificate state you were born on such a date, at a specific time and place, when we know you were alive and growing in your mother's womb for nine months previously.'[4] And so too with death: we take our final breath and are deemed dead although it is a widely held view of many, though not all, that we live on in a different form.

First Death of a Patient

At age eighteen I began my first clinical placement as a young student nurse on a female medical ward in a small teaching hospital. Each morning I would be allocated patients to wash and care for under supervision for both timeliness as well as quality of care. The trolley used for bed-bathing a patient at that time went under such scrutiny I often wondered in hindsight if those supervising me mistook it for a sterile procedure. Though fondly now, some many years later, I recognise their high standards as being beneficial to patient care; that the training was fuelled with fear for the student nurse is just an irony of healthcare.

My first experience of the death of a patient was to occur on that placement, where I would meet and experience the loss of a dear patient whom I would learn from and grow to love. 'Anne'

---

3 Thich Nhat Hanh, *No Death, No Fear.*

4 Elizabeth Lesser, *Broken Open.*

was a woman in her early forties, a religious sister of the Poor Clares order, and my interactions with her would leave a lasting effect on my life. I was routinely assigned the job of bed-bathing her each morning, and each morning she insisted on the struggle of getting her intricate veil on, part of the habit worn by that enclosed order.

As the weeks went by this became the one room I loved to enter, for there in that single room, despite the constraints of time pressure outside on the ward, I lost all sense of time and space. I found Sister Anne's presence enchanting and I was curious about her. Often in the middle of care she would reach up her weak arm and touch my face with her hand, telling me in an altered state of heavenly presence that we were all angels sent to comfort her. She must have been in a lot of pain because as I turned her gently she would quietly groan, and yet at every opportunity she expressed deep gratitude for the care she received. I became somewhat awestruck at her reverence and serenity. Often, as can happen on busy hospital wards, these precious moments of connection were interrupted by the hurried arrival of the nurse in charge, who would appear at the door with a warm greeting to the patient while at the same time offering me a stern look that implied 'efficiency of time'.

As the weeks went by and Sister Anne's condition weakened, I was aware of becoming somewhat attached to her, and often found myself drawn to her bedside at quiet moments when no one was around. Even though she had not spoken in days, and I had listened attentively to the night nurse's report each morning, aware of both her terminal illness and weakening condition, nobody had actually used the term 'dying'. That day

I was oblivious to her pending departure because, as I scurried past her room to report my return from lunch, I was redirected by a colleague who simply said, 'Quickly, we have all been called to attend prayers for Sister Anne'.

As I entered the room I saw candles were lit around her, with one or two relatives standing quietly at the end of her bed and prayers in full flight. Sister Anne had died, and the dawning realisation of her final passing came as an overwhelming shock to me. I had washed her weakened body only that morning and now she was gone. Though those around me were immersed in prayer, I found myself besieged with tears that despite my best efforts could not be muffled. Almost immediately I felt the sudden firm grip of a hand on my arm and I was swiftly ushered out of the room by the ward sister.

Outside the door I was annihilated. 'What is wrong with you? Have you never seen anybody die before?' I was eighteen and had just left home some three months earlier. Rather pitifully I replied 'No' in between sobs, though this was not entirely accurate. I was then sternly told that it was not the nurse's place to cry and in future I should remember that my job was to console the family. Then suddenly she paused, right there in that moment, right in the middle of her berating me, she stopped as though something had shifted within her, and she began to look at me with compassion and empathy. Though no words were spoken I suddenly felt her kind gaze looking down at me.

Then, seemingly out of the goodness of her heart, she directed me to clean the sluice room. It might not initially seem the most ideal place to be banished, but for me in that moment it came as great relief. This solitary task afforded me time and privacy to gather myself, to wipe my wet face, to once again regain composure and breathe easily in the aftermath of such shock. Soon thereafter I re-emerged, dry-eyed and composed, leaving an impeccably clean sluice room in my wake.

Later that evening when I had finished my shift, I did what I realise now might sound a little strange: I stole keys from a ward on the ground floor and having opened a series of doors, I slipped in to the mortuary and found who I was looking for, to say my goodbyes in privacy. For me this was not something scary or strange because as a young child growing up I had always continued to chat to those belonging to me who had died, and this felt no different. Saying goodbye to Sister Anne seemed the most natural thing in the world, something I needed to do, as I would never see her again. Walking into the room to see her at that moment, my only fear was to be found by the living. There was a distinct sweet oil smell in the mortuary and a palpable stillness. Touching her cold clasped hands and looking mournfully at her serene white face, I recall telling her from my nervous heart that I would miss her terribly, and that I would need her help to survive this 'military style' nurse training.

Moments later, I sneaked back out of the mortuary, locking the door behind me and returning the keys, greatly relieved not to have been seen or questioned by anyone. I retreated back to the apartment that I shared with four other student nurses, grateful for that safe haven where we all talked and cried well into the night. It was to begin a habit of a lifetime in my professional career as a nurse, being consoled or offering my own wise counsel to my peers in the absence of any type of formal, structured clinical supervision.

So it was that this quiet religious sister, who had chosen to live her life mostly in silence within an enclosed order, had a lifelong impact on me. In that period of my life during my nurse training, I used to call on Sister Anne in times of stress, particularly around exams. Closing my eyes I would see her veiled white face smiling back at me, gifting me strength and courage at different crossroads in my life.

I developed an idealistic notion of this small order of enclosed nuns who lived beside the hospital where I was training to be a nurse. On night duty we would hear the toll of their bell at four in the morning and, from the small window in the nurses' station, we would watch them stream out into the garden to work. Soon again another bell would toll and they would stream back in again in single file for morning prayers in reverent silence. In comparison to the religious sisters at the hospital whose tough training was being felt keenly by me, I held the Poor Clares in very high esteem. I claimed at the time that in the unlikely event of ever being forced to join an order, it would have to be the Poor Clares. This caused my closest colleagues to laugh hysterically, reminding me of the order's vow of silence, among other things. Teasing me that I would not last five minutes in a silent order, let alone a lifetime, made me laugh too, as this of course held more than a grain of truth.

3

Death in Community

FOR NINE YEARS I worked in community care (the care of people in their own homes by community health and social care services) in Dublin, visiting young families and their new babies at the start of life as well as older people often at the end of life, assessing their needs and tending to their care. When you walk into a person's home you immediately get a sense of who they are, and their environment can provide lots of helpful information. It is a great honour to be invited into the home to offer this care. As healthcare professionals it is good to remind ourselves that we are guests there as it keeps us humble.

Being human means we cannot escape the sadness when a loved one dies. No doubt when our time comes to die, like everyone else we will each individually be hoping for as much dignity and as little pain and discomfort as possible. But in contemplating death we must elevate our consciousness to higher levels than the lower vibration we may operate from in our busy day-to-day lives, in a world that often feels shallow and superficial.

In dying we leave our physical bodies behind. In Buddhist culture they refer to it as 'the dropping away' of our physical form. Whichever way we choose to refer to it there can only be one conclusion: one day we each in turn go back to the eternal world of spirit. We do not go somewhere strange; we merely go back to where we have come from. Understanding this truth behind our existence as human beings and experiencing the spiritual aspect of ourselves in life can really benefit our present-day living. It helps us garner a deeper perspective on our reactions to the stresses and issues that burden us and frequently rob us of the joy of living.

The Wish to Die at Home

I recall one particular gentleman, 'Seamus', who was without family and expressed the wish at every opportunity that he wanted to die in his own bed in his own home. Seamus brought us, his primary healthcare team, into his bedroom to look at the bed. He said he didn't care who was with him, or even if there was no one present, but that it was his greatest desire to breathe his last breath 'right there'.

All support services were accessed including the local hospice team, his general practitioner, the community care nursing services, as well as additional carers. A deeply private individual, it pained Seamus greatly to have what he referred to with great disdain as 'strangers' in his own home but he came to befriend these strangers, and they him.

Human resilience and determination of spirit are two qualities that remind me of this man whom we cared for in community. On one occasion towards the end of his life, Seamus was found on the floor of his small cottage home, semi-conscious and dehydrated. His general practitioner (GP) had to call an ambulance and he was referred in to the local hospice in preparation for his passing. I winced with disappointment for him when I heard news of it from his lamenting GP, whom we all in turn reassured that she had done the kindest deed and taken the most appropriate action, though our collective hearts felt heavy at the time. But I need not have been disappointed for long because within a few hours of this news, the local hospice team alerted me in an alarmed tone that Seamus had gone home against medical advice. Once he had awoken and regained awareness of where he was—in a hospice bed—Seamus took his own discharge and, amidst much protestation from the hospice staff, he called a taxi and left for home.

Though I had just reached my house, this phone call prompted me to turn my car around to visit him. I found him safe and secure back in his own house, curled up in bed saying, 'I want to die here!' I smiled and assured him of the support needed to do so. Though Seamus battled physical symptoms bravely with the expertise of his home care team, he also struggled with the pain of lost contact with loved ones over the years, and we sat with this sadness and regret of his life often in silence.

Seamus had a very kind, mindful and loving neighbour whom he had only recently befriended in his illness. She provided access to us all, so we could tend to him in his home. It was therefore quite befitting, less than a week later, that she had come in early one morning to find Seamus breathing his last, and alerted those involved in his care of his peaceful passing in her calm and loving presence. Though we were just the caregivers, we all stood in his house that morning almost as bereft as anyone of an extended family, for his determined nature and humility had touched us all.

Reflection

To the average person on the street, working with the dying or bereaved may not necessarily indicate a joyous profession, but I am innately drawn to this work as are so many others who have found their field in hospice and palliative care work. Separate from all the organisational stresses known to every clinical environment, I often feel a deep sense of joy in bearing witness to the transformation of suffering in response to compassion.

Quietly and alone to myself, I sometimes consider that if people could really see what happens they would be deeply inspired by the resilience of the human spirit. The ability to witness as well as hold great sorrow humbles me. I often give gratitude for this work that helps me to live my life with greater knowing and appreciation.

Mrs Scott's Hidden Grief

One day I had scheduled to visit an elderly lady, 'Mrs Scott', approximately six weeks after her husband's death. Though aged ninety herself, she had been his main carer. He had struggled with ill health, and for the last few weeks of his life there was a busy train of various healthcare professionals calling on them at all hours. I had remarked that life would be quiet in the aftermath, and arranged to come back to see her, to follow up on her bereavement and assess her own needs now that she lived alone.

Mrs Scott and I sat in chairs on either side of a small fire before the hearth. There was much to chat over: her involvement in his care, his long illness, his suffering, who had attended the funeral and, in good Irish style, who had not. After a period of time a silence came and we sat with it. With the fervour of conversation now passed it seemed fitting to allow space for emotions to arise. And so with little surprise, tears came and Mrs Scott began to cry, and continued to cry, for quite a long time. Still I waited, not wanting to stop or block the avalanche unfolding, and towards the end quietly in my own mind I began to wonder if there was more to this than her husband's loss. Though I had not breathed a word of my thoughts to her, she looked up from her crouched position leaning over the small open fire.

'No', she said, as though she had read my mind. 'No, I am not crying for my dead husband. He suffered terrible in the end and it was a release for him to go. No, I am crying for a baby I lost over fifty year ago. They took my baby away from me, told me to go home, forget about it and go away and have another one.'

Mrs Scott relayed the story of her full-term stillborn baby, whom her late father and husband had gone out into the night to bury quietly, as was the custom at that time. Her now deceased husband, she relayed to me, had never allowed her to talk about it.

This was a profound moment for me as a young midwife and one of the most significant home visits I had ever attended, one that is etched in my heart to this day—this hidden grief held in Mrs Scott's heart for decades, finally being spoken. I was not to know then that the power of this visit would motivate me years later to reach out, to offer healing to those of past generations, to honour the babies who were buried without acknowledgement or ceremony, whose parents were given little or no permission to express their grief and sadness openly.

Suffice to say we chatted well into the evening on all of the events and how she had harboured this deep wound so close to her heart for decades unspoken. Sometime later before I left community care she spoke of laying a wreath at the family plot where the baby had been buried, though sadly the headstone showed no recognition of their baby's burial.

Shortly after this poignant home visit I went on to do further training in spiritual care of the dying. Within a few years I returned to the area, taking up the post of Bereavement Midwife at a large Dublin maternity hospital. After a short settling-in period in my new role, I set off one evening from work, feeling prompted to visit Mrs Scott in her home. I got no reply at her house or her phone, so I liaised the following morning with her GP who had always been very good to her. She directed me to a long-stay residential care hospital and there I found her in a four-bedded ward.

But for Mrs Scott's name in print over the bed, I might not have recognised her emaciated form. I called out to her, knowing her hearing was poor and obviously worsened because by then I was shouting loud enough for the entire hospital to be aware that Nurse Shine was there. Mrs Scott had insisted always on calling me by what she herself referred to as my 'full title' despite the fact that everyone else in community care, including her late husband, had called me by my first name. She sat bolt upright in the bed, delighted to hear a recognisable voice. Clutching my hands she enquired after my whereabouts and the wellbeing of all my family. She was one of the most endearing clients I had ever met.

So I proceeded to tell Mrs Scott of my new job, including the impact of our conversations around her own baby's loss as being influential to my new career choice, and this seemed to please her. What occurred thereafter was nothing short of the Spanish Inquisition: she wanted to know everything about my work and I told her everything. I told her that bereaved parents got to see and hold their baby around the time of death, they got to name and bless their baby, and family members came to meet the baby. I told her about the gathering of photos and other memorabilia such as hand or foot prints, the healing services provided now by the different faith traditions, and the dignified manner in which babies are buried, and that many families bring their baby home the night before the burial.

With all of the updated care practices relayed, all of a sudden the questions stopped. Much to my alarm, Mrs Scott closed her eyes, clenched her two fists and started to bang the bed. I had a moment of personal panic; what had I done in my free flow of information? But right there and then she opened her eyes and fists once more, and announced that she was so happy. 'Phew', I thought. It did not matter that those services were not there for her, she told me, she was just so pleased they were there for mothers now. And that statement just about summed up for me the measure of her character—a warm loving presence concerned always for others.

Mrs Scott died some months later and I was so grateful to her family who sent me her memorial card. As my work in the maternity hospital grew, shelves around my office filled with little babies' photos, and there was Mrs Scott overseeing them all, her tall card peering out from the back of the shelf making me smile always.

Reflection

It was there in community during those poignant home visits that I began to understand the importance of deep listening and compassionate presence and how much of our shared human suffering can be transformed when simply witnessed and held.

Years later, as I embarked on training as a meditation teacher, my awareness deepened considerably. I had often experienced moments of deep awareness in my earlier years; without effort or invitation they would emerge. In more recent years during various meditation retreats, I would recognise that same stillness again, though as soon as I would begin to admire this ability it would be gone. And so the art of 'grasping after' was soon found to be futile in my fieldwork.

Meditation is about accessing a stillness within us, which is a dimension of consciousness that transcends the thinking mind. Often this state may emerge organically without 'trying' to meditate, when you are still or out in nature or simply alert. The more one practices meditation, the more likely one is to have these experiences of simply being. With increased awareness there is a greater likelihood of noticing such moments as they arise. We miss out on so much when we are stuck in the field of thoughts in our storytelling mind. I have learned this for myself and found it to be liberating.

As I had always been an anxious child, I tended to worry a lot. It is not necessarily that I have suddenly stopped worrying, for one does not just wake up and let go of forty years or more of conditioned behaviour. Rather, I notice in sufficient time and can decide to indulge those fears or recognise them for what they are—just fearful thoughts created in the mind—and let them go. I have learned to smile and frequently laugh at myself when I observe this habit. One could say the quality this life skill affords me and my inner world is immeasurable. Many of the Buddhist practices of meditation and compassion that I have learned are now incorporated into my bereavement work which I have found to be incredibly beneficial in helping to alleviate suffering in both the living and dying.

4

Vigil with the Dying

WORKING IN COUNTY KERRY as a night nurse, I felt very grateful to be afforded the opportunity to work with the dying in their own homes. I had left my post of eight years as a public health nurse to pursue my interest in spiritual care of the dying. My new position was temporary work that arose only when there was a need, and for that period in my life this type of work suited me. I would be asked to sit with the dying person towards the end of their life in the family home

Essentially I was a nurse upskilled on symptom management for this job, but equally I was there in my own capacity working through a framework of deep awareness, meditative and compassion practices. I saw this particular role encompassing three main categories of care: provision of physical care and alleviation of physical symptoms, spiritual accompaniment to support transition of fear in the dying person, and support and care of the grieving relatives.

It was almost ten years since I had worked a night shift. Like most nurses, I undertook the usual practical preparation for these visits but at this stage in my life it was important to incorporate my own spiritual practice into this preparation. Before leaving home I would sit for forty minutes or so, dropping into the stillness of my own being to meditate. This practice helped to ground my energy, connect with my own higher self and direct the healing energy ahead of me towards the person I would be called to visit. The support of my own spirit guides and a sense of unseen forces around me afforded me great comfort as I set out for my night's work. I never felt alone and despite the fact that many of the homes in the countryside of west and south Kerry were unmarked, I surprisingly found each home with great ease.

The true art of healing presence begins with a knowledge and belief in its power to touch the wounded hearts of those we care for. Sometimes in healthcare we may feel that we lack words, or struggle to find something to say to try to 'fix' pain and heartache. When we try to fix pain, or when we try to fill silences, it is in fact a distraction to being present. 'Showing up' for the individual or family is in itself a true gift. To be truly present, we must be still. We must begin by breathing deeply ourselves and settling our anxious minds; as we do, our body language may shift. Letting go of what is often referred to as performance anxiety, we must learn to trust and rely on our own innate goodness as human beings to be enough. Care does not need to be complex. These simple yet profound tools are a grounding force that, when engaged, have the power to break down barriers, facilitate healing and allow deep human connections to unfold.

May

There are many cases that come to mind of my time in Kerry, but one call in particular is worth a mention. This elderly client by the name of 'May' lived in the heart of a small rural community. She was a widow and had a large loving family surrounding and supporting her. When I met her the first night I was surprised to find her alert and conscious. She opened her tired eyes and looked me over, enquiring of my background. Her eyes searched deep into the very heart of me, and she scanned my face and scrutinised my actions around the room on that first introductory meeting. I imagine that if I were on my own death bed, I too would do the same to whomever came to attend to me.

Unlike other calls I received, it became evident that May was not actively dying. I was being called upon to sit with her for two nights a week to support the family. On my first night, I was sitting at her bedside and closed my eyes. I became aware of a warm loving presence that seemed to take up the entire space of her small bedroom door. I asked this presence why I had been brought to her at this time. The answer I sensed from that deep moment of stillness was, 'Because she is very frightened'. Having been nervous and afraid most of my earlier years, and knowing fear and anxiety intimately, I have a genuine and heartfelt compassion for those who are frightened. So the answer afforded to me that night by a spiritual presence was deeply compelling. I could work on this with ease and knowing.

If there was any doubt about what I was sensing, at approximately 3 a.m. each night I was with her, May would call out, 'Help, help, help'. Then I would take her hand and move in closer, reassuring her of my presence, and she would quieten again. In this repeated outcry each night I would enquire softly as to the nature of her distress but each night the silence spoke the answer, and I came to see and feel that May's distress would not, or could not, be articulated in words. The comfort of touch and human presence soothed these moments in the early night shifts.

Each morning after the handover to the family, I would return to May's side and bid her farewell. She would open her eyes, dart them around the room and when assured of privacy she would make one simple request: 'Say nothing of what happened last night to the others', to which I would warmly smile and reassure her. Then she would be gone again, eyes tight shut, bidding me safe travel. I came to love and admire this attempted control over her vulnerability, knowing perhaps we might all behave the same in such circumstances.

During one of my early visits, May's daughter shared with me her mother's expressed hope that when she came to die her deceased husband would come to support her passing. This phenomenon is familiar to many faiths. In some shamanic work, prior to our passing over the mythical blackbird lifts the veil between this world and the next, allowing the dying person to see the faces of the people they love who are in spirit.

One night towards the end of May's life, I arrived at her home and her daughter told me something that had occurred. At this point May was sleeping the entire time in a semi-conscious state. While being turned in her bed, she opened her eyes and relayed a conversation she'd had with her husband in spirit. Sceptical and questioning, her daughter sought my opinion, 'Was that the morphine do you think?' At the same time, she wanted to tell me in great detail the sense of peaceful serenity they had witnessed in her mother at that moment. Immediately after May had spoken, she slipped back into an unconscious state. They were some of the last words May spoke to her family before her final passing. Needless to say, I placed more weight on the shared communication with her husband in spirit than the morphine as the source of her serene state.

I often conceded privately to myself that perhaps I should never have been paid for the last night I spent at May's bedside, because in truth it was pure bliss. All remnants of fear had been transitioned. There were no more outcries and I felt a warm and peaceful energy bathing the entire room. Though I was not physically present at her death, soon after that night with all of May's own devoted and loving family present, a very peaceful transition was witnessed. Very often when the struggle of attachments is worked through, a deep serenity bathes over the dying person and they become almost translucent. It is often breathtaking to witness this level of peace in a dying person as they surrender, let go and move closer to Spirit. In truth it is as though they are already experiencing that other world.

Reflection

During this time, living by the sea out on the Dingle peninsula, working as a night nurse to the dying in their own homes, I felt a deep sense of connection to Spirit as well as groundedness. Each night as I set out on these big visits I would drive up through a high mountain pass, connecting with the spirit of the mountain, seeking support for myself as well as for those to whom I was called upon to care. And as the mountain pass gifted me refuge at night, the ocean gifted me another ritual for the returning journey home in the morning.

The ocean has always been for me symbolic of the threshold

where the two worlds meet. So I'd go there to offload to Spirit all or any of the felt energy from my night's work. It was a cleansing ritual, one of deep unfolding. For this, I had a great fondness for a long stretch of beach called Inch Strand. It seemed to stretch for miles and miles, and I could drive my car out onto the sand. It looked out onto the vastly expansive Atlantic Ocean. Always feeling the cold acutely, I did not always get out of the car but frequently sat looking out at the sea with a deep sense of letting go. I would visualise that those with whom I worked, who may have passed over or may be journeying towards that other world, were brought there in spirit with me. Out in the expanse of the ocean they were reflected in the mist that emerged just above the crashing foam of each new wave. I trusted that my Celtic ancestors and the healing energy of the sea were guiding them. Leaving there and driving home felt like the 'handover' had been done.

Difficulty Letting Go

I was called one night to an old country farmhouse in south Kerry. The referring palliative care team informed me that this elderly woman, 'Mary,' had been dying for a long time and repeatedly her family had been called thinking she was breathing her last, yet she continued to live. The home care team was respectful of Mary's process and cautioned me about the family's exhaustion.

Upon entering the home I was met by an array of Mary's adult children, all lovingly tending to their mother and yet the weariness of the extended dying period was evident in their dark-circled eyes and pale demeanours. They had become familiar with the night nurse role but I was new. Hovering quietly in the back of the room, they requested I check Mary's pulse and give them some indication. It was my belief then, and remains today, that assessing the pulse and heart rate is of limited value in estimating the time of death. Dying is a much more complex holistic process than we imagine. But having a huge desire to support them, I did as requested and indicated what I found—a strong heartbeat and regular pulse, at which point they indicated that they would go to bed.

As I stood respectfully outside while each of them said their goodnights, I overheard a conversation from a close friend who was part of the family. Pleadingly she asked Mary not to leave her, saying she did not know how she would cope in her absence. I felt a huge tenderness open in my heart in response to this child-like cry. Intuitively my heart wrenched for this friend's anguish and distress. She took a long time to come through the half-opened door of the bedroom. As she did, I could see tears in her eyes as she called agonisingly back to her dear friend not to leave her, but that they would see one another again early in the morning.

I sat with Mary's friend in the adjoining kitchen and enquired about their friendship. The dying woman had been like a second mother to her and she was really struggling to let Mary go. There was no other companion like her, she told me, and we chatted about the emerging feeling of being left alone. A deep sense of fear of abandonment was evident, indicative I felt of this person's previous life losses which Mary had supported her through. As we sat there, sometimes in silence, other times nurturing and supporting her deep fear of the loss of her closest confidante, something shifted. About an hour had passed and, as the last family member bid us goodnight, I suggested we both sit at Mary's bedside.

As we sat with Mary, much emotion was expressed and a deep

sense of gratitude for their friendship was verbalised. This resulted in a facilitated conversation about letting go of the ongoing friendship. At another level and without prompting, she gave a final invitation for her dying friend to go in peace. When she left for home we embraced gently and she assured me she was going to be okay, and I knew that it was true just by looking at her.

Though still many hours left in the night, I felt in that moment our work was done. It did not surprise me that this older woman died peacefully in her bed an hour or so after I left that morning. The local hospice team had been sceptical when I called to say I did not expect she would be there the following night. They had heard it from several other night nurses for days before.

In the process of dying the senses begin to shut down but it is a widely-held belief even among medical professionals that the ability to hear is one of the last senses to leave us. Mary's case affirmed this for me. It is so important for us all to find the courage to support loved ones in passing over. This is particularly true when we are very deeply emotionally attached. In many cases the one person who never leaves the bedside, the one who wants to be called at even the smallest change, tends not to be present at death. I believe that their absence from the bedside is the last gift they give their loved one and I often consoled bereaved family members of this, only to realise later that I had to take my own advice when this happened for me in my father's passing.

Navigating Death in a Hospital

Although the vast majority of people wish to die in their own homes, the reality is that most die in busy hospital settings.

This was the reality I faced when it came to my own father's passing despite my heartfelt desire to care for him in the privacy of our family home. Instead, after a long illness with Lewy Body dementia, my father was admitted to an acute hospital bed with symptoms of aspiration pneumonia. He died in a seventeen-bedded ward surrounded by lots of elderly people with evident dementia calling out for care, noisy televisions in the background, visitors coming and going, and commode chairs with their accompanying noises and smells all around him. Not dignified, but not without salvage either.

From the moment I looked at him in the hospital bed I knew he was signalling the end. His eyes looked past mine and though in clear recognition, no words were verbally spoken. I knew he was aware I was present. I sat with him, somewhat bewildered amidst the busyness, taking him and all around him in. After a period of time I sought out and approached the nurse in charge to enquire about his care. The nurse rather robotically told me that the consultant he was under would only speak to relatives by appointment on a Wednesday. This was Friday and I knew he would likely not be there come Wednesday but this did not occur to her. About an hour later, even though the body language indicated, 'We are busy on rounds', I hovered nearby observing the team going from bed to bed.

As soon as the consultant and team emerged from behind the curtain of my father's bedside, I nosedived in, much to the annoyance of the nurse in charge. The consultant, upon enquiry of my father's condition, went forcibly into medical mode, bombarding me with blood results and medication management in great detail. After a period of in and out listening, I interrupted as I gestured behind the half-pulled curtain. 'Look at him', I said of my own father, 'the man is dying'. Startled at the directness of my statement, this kind older physician whom I have no doubt was near retirement, looked at my father, looked at me, looked back again at my father, and conceded that perhaps I had a point. He asked me then with equal directedness, 'What would you like to do about it?'

By then my tone had shifted with the acknowledgement of his probable dying. I told the consultant that a single room and access to palliative care staff would be beneficial. The nurse who seemed to have re-entered the consultation told me kindly that no such space existed on the ward. The consultant added that palliative care staff did not take referrals on a Friday, but they would link him up on Monday with the team. Again I knew in my heart of hearts that this would be futile. Seeing this thought on my face, the consultant told me he would write up medication management on his drug chart should he need anything, again conceding sympathetically as he looked towards my father that Monday likely would be too late. I was so grateful they could now acknowledge the imminent events, and thanked them for responding as best they could, late on a Friday afternoon in what appeared to be a busy medical ward, filled to capacity with older patients of whom my father was just one.

Having made my peace with where we were, and opening up to how his transition was unfolding, my younger brother and I alerted the family of his weakening condition then stayed with him late into the night, returning in the early hours of the following morning to be with him. Late that afternoon, when alone at his bedside, I pulled the curtains around my father's bed, sat in a big armchair close beside him and lightly touched his right knee. To my surprise, I suddenly noticed just above his bed a small window looking out from the fourth floor ward onto a vast field and mountain top, with a small forest of trees visible in the distance. I had not noticed it before. It seemed to be our gift to compensate for not having a single room, as no other bed in that ward had such a view.

I closed my eyes in deep gratitude for this connection to nature and began a remarkable journey. I began hearing the hum of the words of the hymn 'Be Not Afraid'[5] as I was certain, from the energy about my father and the haunting look he had given us before closing his eyes for the last time, that I was picking up on fear. Soon after, a vision of the Buddhist centre in West Cork emerged in my consciousness and I saw their prayer flags blowing in the wind in our direction. Almost immediately then my father appeared to me in a vision whereby he seemed much younger and I was older. Transported back in time to our farmyard where we both now stood looking out over the old farmyard gate, gazing out onto the fields of our land, I invited him to walk with me.

We took off on a slow walk up through the fields and there was a lovely tender friendship of sorts to be felt between us, a calm abiding. As we meandered through the fields he stopped frequently, noting all the particular places of relevance to us both, the places where, when I was a young child, he had lifted me over ditches, picked apples from the orchard and gathered mushrooms from certain fields. It was as though he was saying goodbye to

5 Robert J. Dufford, S.J., *Be Not Afraid.*

each field where he had spent his entire lifetime, where he had always been most content.

At each field he examined the grass. At each field he had a treasured memory. He looked out over each field for a long time as we passed by on the old stone path. He stood then at the 'long meadow' for quite a while. His stance here was typical, standing tall and straight, hands clasped behind his back, though before too long the sun shone and he used his right hand to shade his eyes from its bright light. And this then is where I left him—eyes blinded by light, overlooking the long meadow with contentment on his face.

In the next moment I was brought back by the gentle voice of a kind nurse, crouched down to my seat level. She enquired, having garnered my attention, if she could call anyone to be with me. I awoke and realised there were tears streaming down my face. I must have looked quite the sight when she peered in behind the closed curtain to check on us. 'No', I responded, 'I couldn't be happier', which made us both smile. Sitting at my father's death bed, face flooded with tears, meant we both knew I didn't quite mean it literally. Offering me tissues, she asked again if there was someone to call, at which point I conceded to go for something to eat with my younger brother, as the nurses wanted to turn my father's position and tend to his care needs before finishing their shift.

We had not long gone when my eldest brother, who had been busy farming at home all day, phoned us to say he had arrived at the hospital shortly before my father took his last breath and that he had just died. It still felt shocking to hear he was gone. Soon after, I realised the importance for my brother who had been at home with him for most of his life. It was a deserving tribute to their relationship that my father had waited for the farm work to be done, to die in his presence.

I realised that on many occasions in my role as nurse to the dying, I had consoled family members who perhaps were so emotionally attached that their absence from the bedside had allowed their loved one to pass away peacefully. It was now my turn to eat my own words, to digest my own advice, for in stepping away I had allowed my father to take his leave. As we all gathered around the hospital bed, silently I was recalling, with fondness, the warm treasured memory of our walk through the fields, that unique journey, our parting gift to one another.

Loss as the Great Awakener

Often loss is the great awakener and this was my own experience. The sudden, unexpected death of my much loved mother, aged 61, from a massive heart attack, followed soon thereafter by the decline and onset of Lewy Body Dementia in my elderly father and the ending of a significant personal relationship became my own awakener. These three pillars of my life, which I had perhaps taken for granted, all crumbled around me. Life as I knew it had now changed dramatically. I felt very alone and strange. I did not truly appreciate how much these core relationships had supported me until they were lost. There came with time a deep knowing of the unfolding of my own process and the necessity of these losses to bring me back home to myself. Because in truth, within these relationships that seemed to define me, I had lost a sense of my own identity.

Who are we when these seemingly solid foundations around

us die? Often the truth of that answer only arises just there in that moment of questioning. And if we are awake enough to ask this question then we are sufficiently primed to find our own answers. In our bewildered state, right in that precise moment of not knowing, the truth can then begin to emerge.

Left alone with no longer a home to go to or to come from, I had to create my new self. It is and was for me at these pivotal life events that the reality of both life and death could be truly felt and known. I felt acutely in this new dawning that a deeper understanding of life's transient nature became known to me. Sometimes our lives get emptied out in an effort to help us let go of all that we have outgrown. It is a distinct signal whereby unseen forces let us know the play is now over and it is time to come backstage where our true authentic life begins to emerge. There in the darkness the true script of our soul's work is made known to us.

In the aftermath of loss in our lives, it is normal to experience what is referred to as a spiritual crisis. Everything we once believed in is uprooted and the very foundations of our lives are completely upturned. It is as though we are a tree and have been pulled up out of the ground, lifted from the foundations that gave our life strength and a steady base. In this vulnerable aftermath, with all of our roots exposed, nerve lines touch our hearts deeply, sometimes from an unconscious insensitive remark. We get blown around with even a mild wind and in these fragile moments we are often lost, frightened and alone. Soon afterwards as we move further on along the road, prompted by this new wind circling our life, we go in search of answers and truth.

Few can advise us. We are on our own path and it is at

these times that the unseen forces of our lives direct our course. With time we find that our new road, our new path, begins to clear through the fog and there is light again in our lives as we joyfully awaken to what is unfolding out of our grief. We notice that we are on higher ground and have deeper, more steadfast foundations than ever before. Our life's path can be seen clearly on the canvas we ourselves have drawn and coloured. If only we had known, but then that is the risk we take. We can never know how or what may unfold in this invitation to grow spiritually, an invitation that comes disguised as loss and life challenges.

There is another world that lies beside us all the time, and it is the world of spirit that has been quietly there since our birth. But often it is not until we lose someone we love that we go in deeper search of this hidden, unseen world. Many human beings are prompted on to a spiritual quest to seek answers to the truth of life that human minds cannot logically explain following loss. It is in this searching for truth where we can begin to awaken. It calls us into a deeper place in our lives, though in truth none of us would willingly look for painful experiences to bring us onto the spiritual path. Like the physical pain of labour for the mother, these too are labour pains that we must learn to go with rather than resist as we rebirth our soul selves into a new existence. Through the transformation of our own suffering, a deeper awareness and compassion for others often arises, as we travel this collective earthly journey together.

Being awakened to this new reality is akin to being woken up in a new world, a new existence, though nothing of the exterior world is changed. It is oneself who has changed, changed irrevocably, never to be the same again. This may not necessarily be in a bad way, for you have now entered a new reality, into fresh terrain that will most likely weave and grow around you, as you grow into your new life and fulfil a greater destiny. As we garner more and more life wisdom, we can learn to suffer less. This extraordinary truth may seem unfathomable. We learn a new wisdom, we come to see that all forms of attachment create suffering and we may begin to flow more knowingly through life despite what emerges. It is not that we stop hurting or feeling pain, because this is inevitable when we love others, but we have deeper foundations that do not get ruffled to the same degree anymore. As previous losses heal we know we have that reassurance of our own resilience, our own innate ability to return to wholeness.

5

Delivery Suite Induction

After a nine month period of living and working in Dingle, County Kerry, as a night nurse to the dying, I began to feel the onward push and sent my curriculum vitae to the main hospices in Dublin. However, it was 2009 and the country was veering into a recession. The embargo on recruiting healthcare staff had already begun. After several disappointments, finally I conceded to a good friend's advice of applying for a job as a community care midwife. It was a task I knew I could do without difficulty but initially my heart was unsure. I had wanted to continue working at the death bed but life was signalling me towards the birth bed. After some weeks had passed I began to trust my path and wondered if it was time to re-enter the birthing centre again, though not having worked in a hospital for over ten years, it all seemed rather daunting.

I drove up to Dublin having left the majestic views of Slea Head Drive in Dingle in the early hours of the morning. Arriving in Dublin's inner city, I looked around in dismay at what I considered at the time to be a 'concrete jungle'. In truth, arriving there at that moment, I wanted to cry. I protested to the universe, 'How could this be?', as it made no sense to me at that moment in time. The gods in the sky must have been having a right old giggle because I really was most unimpressed.

As I sat in the car outside the maternity hospital looking around and feeling dismayed, I spotted on the back seat the basket I had carried with me on the night shifts. It had a few books in it that I often read when at a bedside, including the *Tibetan Book of Living and Dying* by Sogyal Rinpoche, *Peaceful Dying* by Daniel R. Tobin M.D. and *Benedictus: a Book of Irish Blessings* by John O'Donohue. With nothing to lose and in sombre mood, I pulled the purple book out, *Benedictus*, and asked the late author for a sign. Closing my eyes and opening the book at random, I read the auspicious title of a poem, 'A Blessing for Mothers To Be'. I sat up, intrigued. Scanning the poem I suddenly found a few lines that stirred and shifted my enthusiasm for the pending interview: 'May you be blessed with confidence, and know that destiny minds and guides your life.' I read and re-read those lines over and over in my heart, looked back up to the gods in the sky thanking them for the guidance, and took off to my interview smiling with gratitude and new-found enthusiasm.

It seemed to go extremely well and the three on the panel appeared satisfied with all my previous community care experience and desire to return to maternity care. Positively appraised, I was just about at the door when one of the panel asked if I would not mind answering one more question. With little time to think I readily agreed as she put the question to me: 'How do you feel about going back into the hospital environment to be upskilled on the busy delivery suite for a minimum six-month period?' I took a deep breath, steadied myself and did what is oft done in interviews, I curved on the truth, telling her, 'I'd relish the challenge'. She let me go. Some weeks later when the time came for this induction I wondered if I'd had brain fog that day. The truth was I was terrified. But with life experience, early morning meditation practice and a little bottle of calming essential oils in my back pocket, I embarked on a fearful but deeply insightful journey.

Delivery suites are by and large stressful places to work. With huge turnover, mothers arriving in spontaneous labour or anxiously waiting to be induced, limited bed space, medicalised childbirth, a variety of skill mix on the team and with the safety of both mother and baby at stake, the delivery suite is a high risk area that not everyone is wired to work in. However, during my induction and upskilling on the delivery suite, I could not have hoped to find, let alone befriend, the quality of midwives and healthcare staff who I did meet.

Deeply compassionate women, these midwives were invested in the wellbeing of each mother and baby as well as being mindful of me during my induction. Though initially I was nervous and unsure, many, whom I recall fondly now as I write, handheld me and guided me to find and navigate my hands through the birth canal once more.

Although daunted by being out of the delivery suite for over a decade, I found the work to be deeply rewarding even if the workload was overwhelming at times. For the most part I relaxed into my new role, awestruck, inspired and safe in the knowledge that an experienced midwife manager was outside the door when needed for support.

As the weeks went by I came to see all my old skills as a midwife re-emerge and, with age as well as life experience, a new quiet confidence began to grow. Being with a mother at night in a one-to-one capacity seemed very familiar and comfortable to me and I soon realised why; women in labour are often as fearful as the dying.

It was incredibly rewarding to meet and greet a set of parents and be with them throughout the speedy thirteen-hour shift. Despite the desire of many midwives to stay on after the end of their shift in order to see the outcome of a long labour, crushingly some final outcomes were handed over, as day fell into night and night into day.

The opposite of death is not life but birth, and I have found it to be as much an honour to be present at someone's birth as it is to be present at someone's death. Life is eternal and death is not the fear-filled end that modern day living would have us believe.

Often in quiet moments on a night shift, while labour progressed, a stillness would descend between contractions. Lights would be dimmed and the only background noise was the pulsating heartbeat on the electronic fetal monitor, which was lowered in volume while all was well. In these soft intervals, I was intrigued to find similar questions arising at a birth bed as those that arose at the death bed. 'Do you think it will be long more nurse?' came from the woman's partner in the same manner that 'Do you think it will be much longer nurse?' had come from the son or daughter at a parent's imminent death. The answers, frustratingly, were always the same: 'not sure'. The new soul arrives when it is ready to arrive, and equally the same response at death, the soul will only take its leave when it is ready. There really is no determining it. So much of the inner journeying is unknown that we just have to be respectful to each person and all they must transition through before they finally come in or go out, in either their first breath or their last.

To be present when a soul enters fully into the physical body at birth, and to be present as a soul exits the physical body at the time of death, is both a humbling and inspirational place to be. Ironically, six months into my upskilling on the delivery suite, I would go on to work in that cruel paradox of death at the time of birth, as I successfully secured a new role in the hospital as a specialist midwife in perinatal mental health and bereavement.

Dame Cicely Saunders, founder of the Hospice movement in the early 1960s, famously said, 'You matter because you are you, and you matter until the last moment of your life'.[6] I would often reflect on that quote wondering, 'And what if the last moment of your life happens in the first moments of your life?' I would conclude, 'Then you matter even more.'

6 Robert Twycross, 'A Tribute to Dame Cicely Saunders', Memorial Service, 8 March 2006.

6

Death at the Time of Birth

MATERNITY HOSPITALS are generally seen as places of great joy, happiness and celebration, and for the most part that is true. But given the nature of my new work as a bereavement midwife, I came to see first-hand that maternity hospitals are also full of grief and sorrow. Many mothers are emotional and sad as they grieve the loss of 'normal' birth when their dreamed-for natural birth turns into a complicated and sometimes traumatic emergency delivery. Many mothers too are separated from their often sick or premature infant when their newborn baby is admitted to the neonatal intensive care unit. There are others who come and go from fertility clinics, aching as they experience a deep primitive longing in their souls to become parents. Others leave the hospital from the early assessment unit with news that they have miscarried, often not for the first time. No one sees them as they head for the lonesome car journey home amidst the hustle and bustle of evidently healthy ongoing pregnancies, buggies and newborn babies. Much of my work was now centred on these families, as well as meeting and caring for families whose baby was stillborn or who had died after birth.

The grief associated with perinatal loss is both profound and unique. When an adult dies, we celebrate and honour the life they have lived. But when a baby dies, parents grieve all the hopes and dreams they had held in their hearts for their unborn child, and they mourn all that could have been and should have been. Often parents grieve that they never got to see who their child may have become. Simple things like never hearing their baby cry, never seeing their child's eyes open in the event of stillbirth, bleeds their broken hearts. It is difficult to put into words what is witnessed. All I do know is the ripple effect of that profound shock and sadness is felt acutely by those who experience the loss, their wider family, and also those staff who are present at such devastating times.

Baby Tom Fahey

One particular couple I met for anticipatory bereavement support were the Fahey family. Like many families who find themselves facing the uncertainty of the diagnosis of a life-limiting condition in pregnancy, the Faheys were devastated, shocked, grief-stricken and fear-filled. Our practice in this area of work is to sit with parents at their time of unknowing, to create a space where difficult emotions can be expressed and held in a deeply compassionate manner.

Once fears are explored and guidance on the different care practices that would support them at the different times are outlined, emphasis is always placed on the here and now. The Fahey's baby, Tom, was alive and growing in utero. Support in establishing attachment with their unborn son was emphasised. In the uncertainty of lifespan this aspect of care is important.

Tom's mother was unique because this is where she was at all times, as she would repeatedly say, 'But he's here now'. It was both human and touching. One quiet Friday afternoon as we in the bereavement team were about to head home, Tom arrived. He managed to pull us back in through the ever-revolving door of healthcare work: the one that is led by heart more notably than head. Head tells you it's time to sign off; heart tells you to go back in.

At birth we tried to make Tom cry, to record this on his Dad's phone, but the young paediatrician indicated sadly to me that it would not be possible. Alarmed at his grey colour and poor tone I whispered to the healthcare chaplain to christen him quickly as his parents had requested. They had brought water from the Jordan River that had been specially blessed and we used it as they had wished. At the parents' request, I went to relay the update of his arrival to his extended family in the waiting room. In sombre tone I told them of his arrival, that he was here but very weak. Apparently I looked so sombre that upon leaving them the family considered he might even have passed, but these little babies are hard to gauge. Ten minutes later when I returned to see them again, Tom was bright-eyed, pink, crying, surrounded by all his extended family and being photographed. I thought, this little fella is incredible. Teasing the chaplain I told her the speedy christening had obviously resulted in divine intervention.

Miraculously, little Tom's condition continued to improve, which I ascertained with early morning phone calls to the night staff over the weekend. By Monday we all concluded that he was a potential 'go-home' baby, much to the delight as well as normal anxiety of both his Mum and his Dad. Memory-making had begun in pregnancy, intensified at birth but the day of his departure for home, seeing his tiny little body in the car seat, was the happiest moment of all. His proud parents made their way around the hospital saying goodbye to all who knew him (the whole hospital it would seem at that point), showing him off. All the while I remained anxious to get them into the car, wanting them to have the memory of being at home with their son and fearful that he might not make it.

The 'known' uncertainty of a lifespan has the ability of what I call 'magnifying' life. And this is exactly what Tom's family chose to do—enjoy every waking moment with him surrounded by family who were all drawn in. As I saw them off I had of course no idea that six days later we would meet again in that same car park under different circumstances. Though they went home to a wonderful team of community care supports, they were keen to return to a follow-up appointment with Tom's paediatrician at the hospital, as they lived local to us.

Each day came a reassuring text as Tom's Mum gleefully relayed reports of his progress. She kept us all smiling. On the eve of their return visit to the hospital I got a lovely text to say that Tom was looking forward to his 'date' with his specialist midwife. Again, lots of smiles at the humour of life as I reflected on the speed of his christening at birth, and here he was eleven days from birth doing well at home under the care of two most loving parents, two big brothers and a large extended family.

The following morning, as I prepared my office for the unusually early visit of an outpatient appointment, the phone rang. In between sobs I heard, 'He's gone... He's gone...' from Tom's mother. Tom had died, and I could hear their unfolding sadness, shock and grief. They were in their car with Tom, stuck in heavy morning traffic but determined to continue to the hospital.

Aware that his Dad was driving, I advised them to put on the hazard lights and pull off the road, which they did, into a petrol station in west Dublin. I was by then on speaker phone endeavouring to guide and calm them as I advised them just to simply be with him, to continue to talk to him, to say any last words they needed to say. Although this came across as a very calm 'in control' kind of voice, on the other end of that phone line I stood alone in my office with tears in my eyes as I heard the words, 'I love you my son', from his Dad. It was one of the most heartbreaking yet tender moments I ever shared.

With both parents again expressing their wish to continue to the hospital, I set about arranging supports for them. I asked for their car registration number and told them I would arrange for the Gardaí (Irish police) to get them to us as soon as possible through the early morning traffic. I dialled the emergency services and spoke to the Gardaí, explained my story and got what I suppose was a reasonable reply, 'Ah no luv, that'll have to be an ambulance'. Pleadingly I told them my dilemma, that if I called an ambulance they would be obliged to take them to the Accident & Emergency (A&E) at the nearest hospital where nobody would know them. I told the Garda that this eleven-day-old baby had a terminal illness and this was not an unexpected death. I then told him a small white lie, that I had a consultant paediatrician standing beside me ready to meet them on arrival if they would only oblige us, just this once, on compassionate grounds. My wish was granted.

Once I heard that the Gardaí had reached the family, I hung up with an urgent need to call the paediatrician, healthcare chaplain and neonatal nurse manager of outpatients, and all were present in minutes. Before we knew it the sirens announced Tom's arrival and we met once more at the exact spot where I had seen them off days earlier. The sight of a female Garda driving their car and the united loving family all huddled together in the back seat was a poignant image, one that has stayed with me.

Seeing Tom's ashen grey face and lifeless little body held close to his mother's heart, held lovingly by his dad's embrace, confirmed for the head what the heart was not keen to believe. We adjourned to my office close by where we collectively reflected on the sad events of the morning. His parents said they felt Tom had brought them full circle. They came to this office upon diagnosis and now had returned to where they started after a phenomenal life's journey with their son. As news filtered through the building, all the neonatal nurses, midwives and medical team who had cared for the family came to see little Tom and his parents, and left with tear-filled eyes.

Before long his grandparents and extended family arrived having heard the news. Thereafter the family left to begin the funeral rituals at home. It is hard to go about a normal day's work after such a morning but the care of grieving families called to us from the bereavement ward and so, collectively, we went on.

Later that busy afternoon I got a phone call to say there was a Garda outside my office. Not making the connection and being of nervous disposition, my mind immediately jumped to my recent speeding offences and outdated car tax. I spoke nervously to the Garda by phone, but much to my relief they reminded me of their involvement in baby Tom's care earlier, saying they were leaving something for me to pass on to the bereft parents. That evening after a long day I came to gather my belongings from my office to head home and there outside my office door was a little parcel: a blue teddy bear all bundled up in cling film and around its neck was a gold 'Garda Síochána' medal. It was held on a ribbon similar to an Olympic medal. So I thought to myself that little Tom for all his efforts did deserve an Olympic gold. Engraved on the back of the gold medal were four words for this eleven-day-old baby boy, 'Baby Tom, Baby Angel'.

I smiled, then began to laugh heartily as is often needed in palliative care work, and was really touched to see an enclosed card to Tom's family. It was signed by all the Gardaí who had been involved in the morning's events, including the Garda who had taken the first emergency phone call. And so it was I came to really understand that day how human compassion is innate in all walks of life, and I have held the Gardaí in very high esteem ever since.

I wondered too on the journey home how it is that stories such as these never make the headlines. Little Tom lives on in the hearts and minds of all who met him, in particular of course his own loving family. He lives on also in the hearts and minds of his somewhat extended family, the staff who cared for him at the hospital. Deep human connections unfold in this work of healthcare that we rarely write about, but it is why we do what we do, and with such heart.

Reflection

People of all belief systems share an underlying human component that requires our wholehearted non-judgemental care and compassion. The universality of our spiritual needs as human beings is at the very core of my work and I feel it is important to remind ourselves repeatedly of our shared humanity. There should be no divides among us. We are all equal, and neither inferior or superior to anyone else on this planet. We must try to co-exist with as much heart for one another as is humanly possible, given the myriad of life situations we each face.

Our very existence as human beings in this world means we all suffer. It comes in different forms, for when we experience suffering in our lives it gives greater perspective on how to live authentically in the here and now, with heartfelt compassion for all of us muddling our way through. Though when it is our time to suffer, we may look around at family and friends and think we are singled out, but that is not the case. It was often my experience that prior to their own loss experience people may not have fully appreciated the depth of human suffering others faced. In the aftermath of the experience of loss, our ability to express compassion for another human being becomes heightened. Loss has the potential to humble us, and can bring us back to our good wise selves as we reach out with deeper knowing to others who are grieving.

In recent years working with bereaved families, I would often ask, 'What is your belief system?' or 'Where do you believe your baby is now?' Exploring beyond their particular faith tradition offered me great insight into the readjusting inner world of the person before me. The answer was not always known, but often merely tapping into the deeper awareness of bereaved parents was like opening a fountainhead, whereby a lot would pour out: experiences, previous losses, dreams, altered relationships and the big unanswerable 'not knowing'. This was by far the most common response, and I came to see that not knowing after a major bereavement was very often the best place to be. It can be a time that brings us to our knees but surrendering to that 'not knowing' can often open a pathway to healing.

Many of us are prone in life to being totally caught up in the mundane, controlled by our restless minds, besieged with fearful thoughts that create stories that may or may not be true. It is how we have all become conditioned to behave as human beings. When death or illness arrives in our life, it is like a tidal wave arising out of nowhere. It crashes down upon us with unimaginable force and leaves us on a new and very strange life frontier. There we have to sit for a little while, washed up on that new shore, and take time to survey where life has landed us. From here we gather ourselves anew and begin to reframe and rebuild our new selves. Healing is always possible when we are patient and courageous enough to find our new way in the world.

Sudden Death

I sometimes bore witness to sudden, unexpected and traumatic loss in maternity care services. On more than two occasions the tragedy involved the death of a mother in pregnancy or childbirth, although this was incredibly rare. I often think of those women who entered pregnancy and childbirth unknowingly. The most immense trauma I witnessed was in having this news broken to the partner and/or the woman's own family soon after the tragic event. In all my years as a nurse and midwife I will never forget the enormous sadness of those scenes. They are not my stories to tell for in truth they are the unspeakable, yet these deceased mothers and their families remain etched in my heart forever.

In most other circumstances it may have been the sudden death in utero, or death soon after birth, of a much-beloved baby following a normal happy, healthy pregnancy. Families naturally found it incredulous that these tragedies could happen as they spiralled into shock and sadness so profound. Some clients referred to it as an out-of-body experience, a well-known phenomenon in trauma work. Many mothers, upon hearing that their baby has died, go into a frozen silence while others scream or run in the fight, flight or freeze response. Many too go into an intense state of panic and anxiety. Often I would see energetically that some had quite literally left their physical body—their energetic body would be there, hovering.

As human beings in these moments of enormous tragedy, we are lucky to have a system that hardwires us to survive. Adrenaline surges through us at times of trauma and shock, and helps us to cope. The physiology of stress is quickly felt in the body and individuals become numb and survive as best they can.

Compassionate holding, either physical or energetic, of the mother and her partner can be used in these moments of immense shock and sadness. Remaining present in the face of such suffering, responding intuitively to the individual need in that moment, can be felt as grounding for the person whose mind is spiraling. Being genuine, remaining compassionate and energetically holding all the difficult emotions being felt in these moments, is the healthcare person's most important role, and it matters not their title, only that the person who happens to be there is fully present. It was always my experience when working with mothers and fathers in the aftermath of a major bereavement, that they recalled with minute detail those that were present with them at the time of that shocking and unfolding sadness.

Stillbirth, a phenomenon that in some cases is likened to a cot death or sudden infant death, is a cruel and traumatic form of loss. The lamenting cry of parents as they ache in disbelief upon hearing the words that their baby's heart has stopped beating, reflects the agony in their unsuspecting hearts. The mother in particular in this moment may spiral internally into a sense of dread or fear that she had let her baby down in some way. The distressed mother often silently feeds into the fear that this was her fault, that if only she had come to the hospital sooner. Although the healthcare team tries to offer reassurance and advice, the mother sometimes continues to list all the possible scenarios that could have saved her unborn child from its unexpected death. Mothers are left with a deep sense of remorse and powerlessness as they face an unthinkable reality.

From my experience of offering bereavement support to parents, most particularly to the bereaved mother, a unique feature became evident to me; irrational guilt was felt by a lot of these bereft mothers. Mothers tended to internalise their felt emotions. At some deep level these mothers questioned themselves. Was it my fault the baby died? Should I have come to the hospital sooner? Did my body let the baby down in some way? These were the thoughts that raced through the hearts and minds of these women in the sad and tragic outcomes they faced, so often unexpectedly. After a time, I came to see that no amount of pertinent medical facts or knowledge could assuage this for mothers. Instead I would always encourage them to talk about these thoughts and help them to recognise irrational guilt as just one of the many painful emotions that are part of the grief that needed to be worked through following baby loss.

The deepest sufferings of our heart or spirit cannot be fixed, but in being held and witnessed they can ease. In terms of my recent work, being with people who were suffering, be it depression, anxiety or grief, I have come to see that deeply held emotions, whether openly expressed or merely alluded to, simply need to be sat with. We cannot fix grief or prevent existential distress but we can be present for human beings in a very authentic manner. The use of gentle touch at those moments of vulnerability is sometimes like a release valve, as it bleeds the broken heart of its held emotion without the need to say anything. When someone is suffering and we realise that words cannot reach them, we must learn to sit and use the very heart of who we are as human beings to ease the pain of others. Our beating hearts represent life itself, and in each moment of our living life we are either contracting or opening, just like our heart muscle. So it is at key moments in our lives, at times of great stress, we either contract and then open, or open and then contract. To behave in this manner is to be a true human being. In my work of journeying with families I would see the initial contracting, opening and softening at different junctures.

Creating Memories

With all baby loss, it has become regular practice in bereavement care to hold ceremony and ritual to honour and name the baby who has died. This is a very important aspect of care, and particularly sensitive in the loss of a twin or triplet. In naming the deceased baby, a vibrational energy is created that is held within the family line for generations to come, etched forever in the family tree, openly acknowledged and actively remembered.

Through the altruistic work of bereaved parents in voluntary agencies, the practice of memory-making has been greatly developed and enhanced, and is now deeply embedded into bereavement care in maternity services. Professional photographs, imprints and 3D castings of their baby's foot or hand are examples of memory-making that are shown, in researching the lived experience of bereaved families, to be hugely important in the ongoing bond they have with their deceased baby.

Later on, to continue the memory-making, parents may wish to invite a small gathering of close family and friends to bear witness to a ceremony of remembering. Planting a tree or rose plant, or creating a special place in their garden or local community can help parents keep their child's memory alive. Family members and friends often take their cue from parents in either openly speaking the baby's name or not in the aftermath of loss.

A Father's Treasured Memory

Bringing their baby home when possible prior to the funeral can help parents to further honour their child's memory and can enhance the ongoing parent-child bond through to eternity. One father whose first-born son had died soon after birth, told me that he and his wife were initially fearful at the suggestion of taking their baby home the night before his burial. Afterwards he reflected with me that it was one of their better decisions. He described in the quiet evening at home how he walked through the farmyard, talking with his baby son cradled gently in his arms. He said now he feels every day in his alone work on the farm that he is in fact not alone, for he feels the presence of his much-loved baby boy working with him. The conversation he says continues on, and he talks quietly to his deceased son about all that goes on with the family.

Held in Heart

I would often reflect with bereaved mothers my own philosophy of their connection with their baby in spirit. When mothers would be overwhelmed with sadness on the morning of their baby's burial, we would reflect on finding a location within themselves where they could visualise the memory of their baby residing. I used the following analogy of the human heart as I comforted them on those profoundly sad days of physical parting with their baby.

We have four chambers in our physical heart, but when a mother loses a baby, I believe a new etheric chamber forms. Of course no heart surgeon could identify it physically, but it is there nonetheless. This new chamber is both full and empty at the same time. It is empty, as no other child will ever fill the void that is left in the aftermath of such loss. But equally it is full, for it is here that the memory of her baby resides throughout the mother's lifetime and on into eternity. In an effort to support the immense agony felt, I invite the bereaved mother, as she stands to witness the physical parting of her baby in either a burial or cremation ritual, to place her hand over her heart in that moment, trusting her baby is at peace in spirit, and affirming a special place within her heart where the baby's memory lives on forever.

Placing emphasis on the ongoing bond mothers have with their baby, supporting them to try to understand why this baby chose to come in at this time and helping them find meaning in their loss, is all part of the healing journey.

Loss in Multiple Pregnancy

Loss within a multiple pregnancy, the death of one twin or triplet, is a complex bereavement and requires special care and attention, particularly for the mother. The challenge in these circumstances is the mixed emotions of both joy and sorrow for parents. The tendency of family and friends can sometimes be to overemphasise the need to be joyful, without due consideration for the mother's deep sense of loss too. It is easier for people to share in the joy and celebration of the healthy well baby, while few are willing to share in the parents felt sense of profound sadness.

In the aftermath of loss within a multiple pregnancy, bereaved parents need to be afforded the opportunity to sit and reflect the loss of their baby twin or triplet, allowing in particular the mother to tend the myriad of emotions she may be feeling for the unlived life of this much-loved baby who has died.

Having items of significance to remember the baby and sharing them with the surviving twin or triplet, or older siblings, holds the thread of energy between them within the family. The use of sibling teddies, giving the older children a teddy bear that says 'for my big brother' or 'for my big sister' helps them form an attachment to their baby brother or sister who has died. Awarding older siblings these teddy bears and listening to parents' stories of their close attachment to them is memory-making at its most beautiful.

Sibling involvement is perhaps the greatest way of keeping the baby's name and memory alive. Small children under the age of seven are very connected to that otherworld that lies beside us all the time. Storytelling, artwork and playing to the child's creative imagination about the ongoing existence of their little baby sibling tends to normalise loss for children from an early age and helps them to form an attachment that becomes lifelong. Children are refreshingly honest in such circumstances and tend to say things just as they are, which can make parents smile through their grief and surprise them in the months and years ahead.

Reflection

I have worked with families in perinatal palliative care where parents either continued, or compassionately induced early, a pregnancy that was not viable, and also with bereaved families where there was the sudden and unexpected death of a healthy baby. Everything from that moment is changed for both the grieving mother and father—nothing is the same. It is a watershed moment in their lives. The lens through which life was viewed before has switched as they grieve the incredible pain of loss in that moment, and in all the lonely moments of the weeks, months and years ahead. They change radically. They no longer recognise their old selves as they become new people.

It is a time of great grief and uncertainty as they not only grieve their beloved child but also many secondary losses too. Those who they expect to be there for them may not know how to be, and often this serves to create further angst in their hearts. Yet they meet others who show up unexpectedly, or perhaps they cross paths with people, often random strangers, who have experienced this loss too and come to help and befriend them.

Often suffering intensely can be the doorway into a new life, although it is a very painful rite of passage for those who lose someone close to them through death. Experiencing a diminished sense of ourselves through loss is humbling but by not resisting this painful journey, a new and deeper sense of who we are at source can emerge. We often have no perception of our true life's purpose up until the point where life events result in the shell of our former life being hit hard and cracked open. As a result of loss we become bruised and wounded, but we reshape again and in the process thereafter we often re-mould into a new sense of ourselves. Often as a result of our own woundedness, we may shift from individual concerns to an awareness of all human suffering. This shift in our awareness tends to result in an even deeper compassion for our collective humanity.

Rainbow Baby

In working with bereaved parents I always have a deep respect for their own individual choice in terms of care, ritual and service. I never assume any right to be present with them in the birth and death of their much loved baby. I have to be invited in on that individual journey, and remain sensitive and intuitive to their need for privacy as well as being there to support them at fearful moments. When this journey is shared, an everlasting bond occurs that often sees one invited back in on their next journey of subsequent pregnancy. The midwife, doctor or neonatal nurse present with them during this time become part of the narrative of their child's memory. This is unique to palliative care in maternity services versus end-of-life care in a hospice because, very often, parents will return with a new pregnancy a year or two later, albeit with much anxiety, and meet again the faces of those who knew and cared for their deceased child.

Collectively, we acknowledged the ongoing sadness while at the same time, after a stress-filled pregnancy, we felt very grateful to be on the continuum with these families, to help celebrate and share in the new joy. This often reminded me of the analogy that joy and sorrow are but two sides of the same coin. Many parents were fearful that because of the new baby, friends and family might assume their grief was over and stop talking about the child who had died. What often occurred was that parents would grieve afresh, as the new baby reached milestones that their other child never did.

It was always such a privilege to be invited in to meet the new sibling, referred to by some bereaved parents as 'the rainbow baby'. We would always talk openly about the baby who had died. This is, I believe, the reason parents would often send for those of us involved in their care, to visit and share with them their complex emotional responses. When I came invited into such rooms on our delivery suite or postnatal ward, I would warmly welcome the new baby, and in a whisper gently ask the newborn in my arms, 'What news have you from the spirit world?' from your big brother or sister, as most parents needed to link both these worlds.

Reflection

The resilience of the human spirit and the wave of love that ripples from these babies' short lives never ceases to inspire me. Watching parents go from, very often, a much-contracted fearful state to almost a lotus-flower opening is heart-warming. Bereavement sessions in the aftermath of such events are an important opportunity to reflect the lived experience of parents, allowing them time and space to heal some of the woundedness in the months and years that followed. Years later I would see that some parents had not only survived the traumatic event of their child's death, they had often expanded as human beings because of their experience. This phenomenon is referred to as post-traumatic growth. They evolve and grow, having had their hearts broken open by a love they never imagined possible. One mother, in the painful aftermath of losing one twin after a lifetime of just five days, remarked after his passing that she had never known love like this and could never have imagined at the start of their journey how much she would love this tiny soul gifted to her for such a short time.

Gathering to Remember

I was invited to give a short address at a remembrance service in memory of babies and children who had died. As I sat outside the venue in a friend's car, I kept checking with her that we were at the right church as the age profile seemed to me to be at odds with a maternity care service; many older people were making their way in slowly. She assured me we were and that these were parents who had experienced the death of a baby or child many years previously, whom she affectionately termed 'our long-ago bereaved'.

It is always daunting, as well as humbling, to be asked to speak at such events. I had woken at five o'clock on a couple of mornings during the preceding week, thinking about these bereft strangers whom I had never met. I believed that attendance for many at such an event would take courage to simply show up. I held them collectively in my heart in meditation. As I did, I found my heart swell with universal love as well as hope that in some small way they would each receive healing for their hearts in the gathering together with others. I knew or felt that it was perhaps not words that would reach them on that day, so I held the intention of healing love in my heart as a more powerful tool instead.

I had been asked to sit by myself in one of the front pews, and took my place somewhat nervously as the church began to fill. All of a sudden an older lady with a walking aid bustled in beside me on the outside seat. She needed to be able to see the priest, she told me, because she had poor hearing and if she could see him that might help her understand what was being said. After a few moments of settling herself, she turned to me and whispered in a low voice, 'It is his anniversary today'. She told me what age her son would have been that day had he not died. There was a depth of soul in this small-framed woman. The power of what she had just shared with me touched my own heart and quieted my mind from the developing anxiety as I sat there. A gentle touch to acknowledge what she had just shared was all I could do as I looked at her face, aged by life in all its wisdom. Soon after, she murmured again, 'A bad tide carried him'. Well these words ricocheted inside my head as I envisioned the scene she might have lived through, imagining the pain she must have felt then and now. She repeatedly said in our brief meeting that it was her faith and belief in the afterlife that had helped her survive. It was also evident the pain was lifelong. She was steadfast in her belief of meeting her son again when she herself died and this provided her with enormous comfort.

Later she introduced me to her husband, and as I took my leave we embraced lightly to acknowledge our poignant meeting that day. There were others too who touched me, younger couples with small children who were evidently newly bereft. I wondered, did it comfort them to see so many older people present, years on from their loss? Would it help them see and understand from the older population present there that the bond with their deceased child lives on?

But it was one other scene that rendered tears to my own eyes, and that was of an older man, I imagined in his late seventies or eighties. He was one of the last to present a glass tea light holder at the end of the candle procession, which was the main feature of the service. He proceeded up the centre aisle with an evidently arthritic left hip and held that candle with such an intense grip: for a moment I was afraid the glass his two hands clung to might actually break. I wondered what painful lost memory he held in his heart. He handed it over and, as he limped his way back to his seat, he used the sleeve of his shirt to dry tears from his face. So now each time I light my own glass tea light holder that we were invited to bring home from that service, I think of him especially with healing love. In doing so, I hope too they are all being guided towards a deeper sense of connection to their loved ones in spirit.

Reflection

The greatest source of human suffering is often the inability to face or manage difficult emotions. We were perhaps not tutored well in this necessary art form. When we repress difficult emotions repeatedly, it can affect our mental health and wellbeing. Being with or befriending difficult emotions has many advantages. Whatever is present in your inner world, whether it is an awareness of sadness or guilt or fear, simply by naming it we give it less of a hold over us. We can look somewhat more objectively at what is happening moment by moment in our lives by being aware of what is present.

An analogy often used in mindfulness practice for the 'tend and befriend' approach for difficult emotions is that of a waterfall. When we stand directly under the flow of water we are likely to be drowned or at least overwhelmed in trying to catch our breath. The alternative is to step back from under the direct flow and stand behind the waterfall. In stepping back we can still feel the spray of water but we are less likely to drown in it. It is the same when we use this approach in dealing with the difficult emotions in our life that tend to overwhelm us. We can take a step back, so to speak, and look at these difficult emotions more objectively, and name what is present.

Naming the difficult emotion, be it sadness, fear, guilt or anger, can be freeing. It brings a deeper awareness to what is going on in our inner world, what thoughts are fueling the felt emotion and where we are feeling its energy in the body. Breathing into this area of the body with compassionate awareness can often ease our distress and begin the healing process. In the end we come to realise a fundamental truth—we are not our emotions; they are simply part of the human condition.

It takes immense courage to turn towards painful or difficult emotions in our life. Our greatest fear is that in facing them we may fall apart. But falling apart may not be as bad as it sounds. Sometimes we have to fall apart in order to piece back together the remaining fragments of our somewhat broken lives. The richness, wisdom and newfound awareness that may emerge from such dark moments are often hidden gifts, just like the analogy in the poem 'The Guest House' by Rumi,[7] whereby he invites us to open the door of our lives to all the difficult visitors who may come, 'joy, sorrow, meanness, depression'. Rumi encourages us to treat these guests honourably and to 'be grateful for whoever comes because each has been sent as a guide from beyond'. It is not so easy to understand the hidden gifts in the early raw acute stages of grief because in truth we are too near our loss to see these. We have to feel into our loneliness and vulnerability before the gifts arrive sometime later. Holding hope for the transitioning of our suffering into meaningful living[8] is an important seed to plant in the brooding mind in the aftermath of loss.

7 Barks, C. *The essential Rumi.*

8 Danai Papadatou, *In The Face of Death.*

A Bereaved Father's Reflection

I distinctly remember one father who had not been vocal in the pregnancy. In fact he sat in silence during most of the antenatal sessions where the anticipated loss of their baby soon after birth had been medically diagnosed and, in so far as was humanly possible, prepared for. Six months after the death of his baby girl, which occurred just minutes after her birth, he phoned me saying it was her six-month anniversary and he wanted to make an appointment.

Though evidently heartbroken he had come specifically to tell me his experience of their baby daughter's birth and death. He described a moment in the delivery suite theatre where he looked around at what he referred to as 'all these random strangers, hidden behind masks and gowns', most of whom he said he had never met before and most of whom he knew he would most likely never see again. He told me when he saw 'tears in their eyes for his little girl' something erupted inside of him and in that moment he was utterly proud of his beautiful daughter as he held her tiny frame in his arms. That she could come into this world for such a short period of time and have an impact at that level helped him enormously. Her life had been deeply meaningful, though her legacy not yet written, for it was too soon from the loss. The experience, he said, had changed him utterly, and there was no need to articulate that this was in a good way as it was so clearly evident. He drove all the way to Dublin to share this with me, to tell me how his contracted heart had been opened in the shared human experience. It had not been easy for him to put his experience into words. There had been a lot of expressed emotion before those words gushed from him, as we both sat patiently with its unfolding.

It was a poignant session, and I was deeply impacted by his gesture of coming to talk with me. I stood with tear-filled eyes as he firmly shook my hand and asked me to give his gratitude to those staff members. It was his deep humility that I remember most. Of course I knew instinctively he would not be back, for in truth he had no need to seek support. He had in fact supported us enormously in the essence of what he shared. For no theoretical knowledge or academic training could have been as effective as that one session learning about what is really important in end of life care—human kindness.

Reflection

It is liberating to 'open the door and invite in' rather than the old approach of covering up or denying our feelings. This old approach does not dispel pain, and it may impede our potential to transition out of suffering and find new meaning again in life. Often there is a risk when we repeatedly repress emotions—one day they may return disguised as a depression. Exploring compassionately each individual's own responses and coping mechanisms is an aspect of my work. In grieving there is no right or wrong road, but a middle path.

Grief then must be seen in its rightful place. It is different from depression. There is no taking a break from depression, whereas grief comes in waves. In between those waves of grief a person can manage to surface from the sadness, take a deep breath and regain some functioning. Yet most people who find themselves in the throes of grief are full of fear. They are frightened that if they allow themselves to feel into the emotions of that grief, they may go into a deep dark depression and never come back out.

After his wife died, the author C.S. Lewis journaled about his grief and began the resulting book, *A Grief Observed,*[9] with 'Nobody ever told me that grief felt so like fear'. And that is exactly what grief feels like. It is a lonely journey for which there is no set map or signposted route, but rather a seemingly endless road. However, we often meet people along the path of that lonely road who help direct us when we have gotten lost or stuck on our way. I often use the analogy of grief as a cloud of energy; it descends without warning, often at the most inopportune times and almost always without invitation. But when we can find time and space, and allow this grief to wash over us, it can be life-giving. Though initially we can feel utterly exhausted and depleted by the emotional release after such a visitor, we can also feel lighter.

Humour in Grief

One day a bereaved mother arrived at my office for an appointment. As we sat she started to sob loudly with grief. She felt the pain of loss of her tiny baby girl acutely. In between sobs she told me fearfully how her husband had advised her perhaps not to cry too much on this occasion, lest the hospital staff think she might never recover. Well we both had a wry smile at that one. And as we sat there through the tears she looked up at me from her crouched-over position and told me with a tear-filled face, 'This grief is hard work'. 'It is', I affirmed, and smiled. She smiled

9 Lewis C.S. *A Grief Observed.*

back and then she laughed, so I laughed, and before we knew it, we were both peeling with laughter. It was a most releasing session on grief. Late in her next pregnancy, when we met again in the delivery suite under happier circumstances, she reflected on the previous loss and the pain and sadness, then recalled too the lighthearted moment we had both shared that day and its healing effect.

Sometimes we just need a space where no mask is worn and where we can be our frail old selves. In that authentic place of owning our brokenness as human beings, often the greatest healing will happen. Colleagues would sometimes enquire whether that was laughter they heard emerge from my office during a bereavement session. Their perplexed faces amused me, and I had to explain that sometimes joy emerged amidst the grief but one only had permission to laugh when one had been there to hold the deepest of pain too.

Love Disguised as Grief

Once I saw a couple who, only weeks before, had experienced the unexpected death of their full-term baby in the womb, just hours before a planned caesarean section. Their grief as they sat in the devastation of the loss of their much longed-for baby was immeasurable. And so late one Friday afternoon, in response to a call, I offered them my emergency appointment. It was a big session as they were reeling from shock with evident anxiety and trauma symptoms.

I had, of course, no cure for any of their difficult and held emotions, so we sat with the expressed fears of where they were in that moment. We had connected at the time of their baby's stillbirth. I had witnessed their expressed grief of this shocking diagnosis and was actively involved in their care during their inpatient stay. We reflected on how perfect their baby boy was and the precious time they had spent with him in the hospital as well as their own home where beautiful memories had emerged for them unexpectedly.

As we concluded our session, I talked with them about being kind and gentle with both oneself as well as with one another. I talked about the need to rest, to allow themselves to come back into their physical bodies and to nurture and nourish themselves at every level. Seeing them off at the lift I turned back into my office to sign off their parking ticket to avoid them having to go through the main hospital where they had such traumatic memories. Upon my return to them, the adjoining door had closed and through the small glass panel I saw the Dad gaze lovingly at his partner who was burdened with so much grief and angst, and placing both hands around her face he gently kissed her.

It was a most tender moment, interrupted only when they became aware that I was standing still inside the adjoining corridor allowing them quiet time together. They smiled apologetically as I came through the door. I was grateful, I told them, to have been witness to the love and tenderness they shared at such a vulnerable time. Many people misinterpret bereavement work, and yet incidents such as this are frequent. I bear witness to so much love disguised as grief.

As I left work late that Friday evening it was with a lightness of heart, aware of the rawness of their grief but acutely aware too of the wonderful gift of love. I felt enormous warmth in my heart, and at times when my workload becomes heavy I think of them and many other such tender moments where I quite literally stand still honouring the love shared between human beings. It is healing to hold onto these precious moments in one's heart, especially in busy clinical environments.

Sometime later we reflected on their baby's short lifetime and the ongoing bond and connection they felt with him, from the memories shared. The search for meaning in his short life was ongoing as a deeper questioning arose in their hearts of why he came to them at that time. With most bereaved parents their individual child's legacy gets richer over the years, as the bond deepens. Exploring our shared human existence and how we evolve and grow through each lifetime is sometimes what emerges in these reflections.

In their son's memory card they used beautiful and poignant words from the poem, 'The Stolen Child',[10] by the late Irish poet W.B. Yeats, depicting perhaps the spiritual path and destiny of the spirit of babies who don't incarnate into the physical realm for reasons so often beyond medical science:

Come away, O human child!
To the waters and the wild
With a Faery, hand in hand,
For the world's more full of weeping than you can understand.

---

10 Yeats, W.B. *The Collected Works of W.B. Yeats.*

7

Maria's Interview on Birth

WHO IS MARIA and how do I reflect this presence amidst my stories? I was referred to her some years ago by a very wise friend. Maria lives life from a very elevated level of consciousness, with ample awareness to function at the physical realm while being in tune and in direct contact with Spirit most of her waking hours. I was initiated by Maria into the higher levels of the Japanese healing art form of Reiki, which allows healing energy to be channelled and transmitted through the fingertips and voice. I was also initiated into the Sacred Grace and Divine feminine energies within the first year of meeting her. Aside from workshops I return to her for sessions in a wide variety of circumstances. On each occasion she would examine through her clairvoyant vision the underlying issue shown to her by the spirit guides. She has always been reliable and is upholding of all that is good in humanity in her communications to me through Spirit. Working at a very highly evolved state of consciousness, she helps make sense of the spirit world for me, in all that I could feel but not yet see. Being highly sensitive in nature I frequently called on her assistance, describing all of what I was feeling acutely in my body, and she in turn would help me understand and heal that which caused me discomfort or pain.

Sometimes I would need to discuss a situation with Maria and she would speak to the spirit world and offer me guidance. These insights were life-giving and would often create noticeable change in the situation I was struggling with. She is incredibly helpful to me in understanding all that goes on that we do not see through human eyes. Though my own intuitive ability and high sensitivity had been dimmed down in childhood, it was re-awoken again through my training with this mystic. Maria allows me access to spiritual understandings that help both myself, my loved ones and those whom I care for very deeply. I am grateful to Maria and all my teachers who help me understand all that I feel and sense and sometimes see.

In one instance I had held a baby whom the medical team had affirmed would die soon after birth. The mother had already experienced the loss of a baby in childbirth before, and the overwhelming fear of revisiting that held trauma led her to resist the suggestion of being with or holding her newborn daughter as she died. The avoidance of pain was compassionately held for this fear-filled mother and despite input from individual team members in support, love and guidance, her fear could not be overcome. So with support from the midwife in the operating theatre that day, as a team we did for this mother what she was unable to do on this sad day—we held her baby girl as she died.

For days after, I felt incredibly weary and a heavy sensation pervaded my physical body. My eyes seemed lost and I had a deep sense that all was not well. With guidance, Maria invited me to visualise the spirit of this baby being supported to transition to the light. I felt peaceful and calm almost instantaneously. As Maria facilitated the spirit of this baby to feel her mother's love, as the mother perhaps had longed to do, the spirit left the physical plane in peace. The spirit of this little baby had hovered until then as her bereft mother, consumed with fear of the pain of separation, had shut down emotionally and spiritually, unable to connect with her baby.

When I met this mother again I assured her that her child had been held, loved and supported. Though she went from our bereavement session with tear-filled eyes, she was grateful for the reassurance and connection felt and shared.

I learned hugely from Maria and met her regularly in Dublin as well as visiting her for spiritual training events and retreats in her home in France. For the purpose of this book I arranged to meet her to ask questions about the transitional periods of pregnancy and childbirth in terms of knowing what is happening at a deeper level of consciousness.

In terms of spiritual midwifery, I sought her wisdom on the spiritual journey of a mother in pregnancy and childbirth. As a person of gifted psychic ability, some of what she details may at first seem far-fetched but having seen the results over many years I can no longer argue. Scientific evidence limits us to only the visible, yet life as we know it is, in fact, multidimensional. The more open and aware we are, the more we come to recognise a truth when it is spoken.

Here are Maria's responses to some of my questions:

> As a spirit is coming towards a woman and wants to come in, the mother-to-be, if she is very sensitive,

can become aware of this and begin to feel it. Often a woman will sense something and feel someone around her but she perhaps cannot articulate what she senses. Though often at odds with the woman and her partner's practical discussions on family planning, women have often commented to me in my work that they just sense another child and I confirm for them what I see, often that yes, there is a spirit who is around her, in her energy field. Through the pregnancy an entire new spirit comes and downloads right through the mother. Often if the energy body of the mother is out of balance the pregnancy may end in miscarriage and the spirit does not come in. In other circumstances the spirit may wish to only come in for a short period of time and the mother is almost just holding that spirit lovingly during this brief period. The spirit will be able to see the mother most suitable to either its short or lifelong journey.

A couple of days before a mother goes into labour there may be a sense or feeling for that mother that she is herself again. During the pregnancy the spirit of the baby is interwoven into the mother's aura with a felt sense of someone being with her, which now of course there is. Once the prompting of the sensation of being herself again occurs, then a signal is sent to the baby in the womb. The baby starts preparing for imminent separation and this is usually signalled thereafter with signs of early labour.

The psyche of a mother-to-be undertakes a huge

> spiritual journey, though very few are aware of it. In the first stage of labour as the body opens up with each contraction, the spirit of the mother starts to travel outward, in the same way that some people astral travel at night in their sleep. The mother's spirit goes out, out beyond her physical body, beyond the realms of the physical world, she travels far off into the cosmos, all the way out beyond the earth plane. She is at this time calling to the spirit of her child from wherever it has ever been or ever will be throughout history. She begins to call this spirit towards her. It is like a big sonar as her consciousness vibrates with the etheric message 'come to me, come to me' as she gathers every aspect of that spirit towards her. And this goes on all the way through labour until she reaches the 'black velvet', the nothingness. She knows she has called forth her child from deep beyond the cosmos and everything is now complete. It is at this moment that she is deemed fully dilated and enters the second stage of labour.

As Maria enters into her 'second module' detailing for me the journey of the psyche in the second stage of labour, I become aware of the evident emotion in her voice, prompting me to look up from my intense note-taking and recording of the interview. I see that the felt emotion in her voice is matched in her tear-filled face, and I realise that she has shifted from 'this is what happens in general terms' to 'this is what happened to me'. She is recalling her own birthing events and very few mothers have the psychic ability to be conscious of all that goes on at this pivotal time. I am touched by her intimate sharing and sense the emotion of her story is as important as the specific details.

> At this time the mother walks the journey of her child's life. She sees and feels everything that will happen to that child, and deep within her soul that mother carries the cellular memory of the events seen by her. Having witnessed the events that her child is likely to experience in this lifetime she acknowledges this and stores it in her psyche. She has contracted to bring this child in and as a mother she is deeply intuitive of her child's needs. We ought to listen when a mother expresses a concern about her child. We must awaken again to trusting the mother's innate and intuitive knowing because the imprint is within her since childbirth. All your life you have a feeling that someone is with you, that you're not really alone. That's true because the person who accompanies your life's journey is an aspect of your birth mother. She has done the whole journey with you in spirit before your birth.
>
> After birth when the baby is born there is tremendous elation. The reason for this, beyond the obvious delight, is because everyone is still in the spirit world. All those who are truly present at the event are in that other world that lies beside us all the time but we cannot see. Thankfully the following day the mother starts to feel physical pain,

which pulls her back into her body energetically, which is necessary. The spaced out feeling has passed because a mother can't stay in spirit. On the third day all the emotions of the journey of the psyche are finally released in the mother's overwhelming state of exhaustion at every level—physically, emotionally and spiritually.[11] The mother has come from the Omega chakra which, in the energy body of eastern philosophy, is the pure divine feminine. The expansion of the divine feminine occurs for women following childbirth and is what gives mothers a deep sense of empowerment from their experience of transitioning into motherhood. Birth trauma denies this to some women. Yet with holistic support this too can be healed.

In the weeks and months after her own childbirth experiences, Maria describes something very strong passing through her as she released more and more of her child's spirit into its physical form. Though for most mothers this is an unconscious process that goes on and is rarely experienced knowingly by the mother, it happens for all mothers and babies, she assured me, and includes those who give birth through caesarean section.

Seeking her wisdom on what occurs for the mother whose baby has died, Maria recounts compassionately that this is the greatest love of all. The mother will have most likely contracted in the spirit world to hold this child for the period of life it chooses. To have a

11 Author's note: as midwives this aligns with our 'hormonal decline theory'.

baby who at an unconscious level you know and understand will not survive, but still contract to conceive and love, is reflective of the pure love of a mother's heart and spirit.

The mother may have intuitively known that this would come to pass, and she may even comment on a sense of knowing because she has walked this child's spirit journey with them. In a mother's heart and psyche this is utterly painful, yet she concedes at some deep level to fulfil her soul promise to the spirit of this child.

On a practical level one very important piece of advice that Maria insists on sharing is the importance for women to have their back realigned at six weeks post-delivery:

> The mother simply must have her back aligned. It is essential to her recovery and wellbeing. Amatsu is the gentlest form of re-alignment as it is in tune with the energy body, but equally cranial sacral, osteopathic or chiropractic methods will serve a similar function. As a mother's pelvis expands in preparation to give birth, her base chakra at the root of her spine is affected and this affects her mental health and wellbeing.

In other words, the safest route to maintaining sanity in the aftermath of childbirth is to get your back fixed!

> Acknowledging the need to realign the spine, it is important to fully understand that if left unresolved then physical health issues will manifest. The mother's immune system and also her circulation will

be compromised. Drive, ambition, energy and mood are all impacted when the base chakra is closed. This in turn affects the neck which may manifest as poor sleep, no ability to focus or concentrate and a general sense of no clarity, 'can't see the wood for the trees' phenomenon. The crown chakra at the top of the head closes down, and within the energy body of the mother there is no flow of Chi and the mother withdraws into herself, feeling alone, disconnected, sad and depressed. In the distress of knowing they are not well, mothers become primal in their instinctive protection of their baby. Therefore the mother presenting with a heightened state of anxiety regarding her baby should be listened to, and should receive a holistic assessment that incorporates all aspects of her being. The root cause of the anxiety needs to be examined compassionately.

Realignment of the physical body after childbirth utilising holistic treatments is common practice in Eastern philosophy and holistic medicine. In these cultures mothers are encouraged to rest and are nurtured mindfully. They are afforded more respect for the truly amazing experience and the alchemic process of birthing a child into the physical realm.

In all contexts of life, both the masculine and feminine principles must be in equal balance. When one is dominant there are repercussions. Here in the West we have come to imply to women to be 'up and out there' perhaps too quickly, without support or

> acknowledgement of the huge reprogramming that occurs in the birthing process. The masculine drive predominant in our western society has not served women well. Women need to be nurtured and cared for sensitively. We are emotional beings. There are women in society today for whom childbirth began a lifelong struggle with low mood and depression. We need to ensure that our masculine overdrive at this time is rebalanced for, as a society, we have subtly turned women into great men. It is time to honour our feminine principles and work harmoniously to right this imbalance, and garner respect of both sexes.

Maria went on to discuss the unique type of loss experienced for the baby who loses a sibling in utero. For example, loss of one twin within a multiple pregnancy. She talked about the baby's first attachment to its sibling being severed and the impact that has on the live-born baby's attachment system resulting from this loss. I would therefore talk to parents about the need to facilitate a strong connection to this baby (surviving twin) in early life, perhaps utilising attachment parenting to support the surviving twin or triplet. Without intense nurturing of the emotional wellbeing of this baby, he or she may go on to have issues with self-esteem, as energetically the solar plexus has been impacted in the loss and separation. Holistic treatments such as energy healing or craniosacral sessions as well as attachment parenting can ease the baby's distress, which is frequently misinterpreted as infant colic.

When a mother loses a baby, Maria explains that, 'An aspect of the mother goes with the child and another part of that mother's own being is downloaded from spirit'. She continues:

> When we incarnate we are but one-tenth of our spiritual selves on this earth plane. When a mother loses a child, that aspect of the mother, the one-tenth of the mother's spirit, goes with the child and another is downloaded, so mothers are changed irrevocably after. Women need to be nurtured and supported to understand that their child is not alone. Even if she had conceived for just a few weeks, a full spirit actually comes in. Mothers need to understand that they may have contracted to bring this child into the world at a very deep level, knowing this child might not survive. And though society openly acknowledges that a mother's love is the greatest love of all, the love a mother has in her heart for a child who dies, and that of a father supporting the woman and child, supersedes this love, as it is the purest love of all.

As we struggle to understand why these sad events happen in our life, we must remind ourselves continuously that it is most often beyond medical science. Often the spirit of the baby may not wish to come in at this time and yet the overwhelming love the child feels is often so healing that it gives them the ability to reincarnate in another lifetime in full. The grief experienced by the parents is felt as pure love by the spirit of the baby at that time. My own belief is that these babies choose their parents in accordance with their chosen short lifetime and that their experience is to feel loved forever.

Mothers trying to conceive again may benefit from Maria's advice:

> Getting their back aligned to balance the chakra energy field of their body will bring them back to feeling themselves and can deal with the new archetype of the mother they have become. Even if the baby does not survive, the mother is always a mother once she has conceived. If their physical body or inner strength is weak they may need energy healing through to the base chakra or solar plexus region to ground them and heal self-esteem issues to facilitate conception and attract perhaps a new spirit to them. Women have the divine feminine ability to draw towards, to call forth a spirit into this world, and must go deep within themselves to find this truth. This primal earth ability of 'drawing towards' by the psyche of the mother is inherent in all female bodies but must be re-learnt and respected. Mothers need to go in deeply into a meditative state and call in the spirit of their much longed-for baby. The mind, ego, have no power here; it is the call of the heart that has the power. Women who are open and aware may sense the spirit of a baby around them and connecting with this will facilitate conceiving.

Despite our very rich tradition in caring for the dying in Ireland, we denied many families the opportunity in the past to acknowledge and grieve the child they had both loved and lost. I often seek wisdom from Maria. I talked to her about the many unmarked mass graves all around our small island where it is known these babies are buried. She had something warm and reassuring for me to reflect on:

> Since the dawn of time there have always been good people on this earth who would have been aware of these burials. They would have offered prayers and lit candles for these mothers, fathers and their babies.

These words said with such deep knowingness had an immediate effect on me as she assured me that those in the spirit world would have supported these babies in their transition back to light. She believes we simply have to trust that each child was prayed for quietly by good people who knew what was happening.

8

Maria's Interview on Death

HAVING GARNERED much insight into birth, I reached out again to Maria, my mystic teacher, to seek her wisdom on the spiritual process of death, dying and the afterlife. I offer you now her insight and wisdom with this final interview asking her how best we can help those whom we love when they come to die.

> To help someone, or a loved one, to pass over, one of the most helpful things we can do is use prayer or meditation. It is always helpful to use prayer when someone is passing over and it is better to say prayers that have been part of a tradition. It doesn't matter what the particular tradition is, but prayers that have been said by millions of people for thousands of years result in those prayers being very potent.
>
> Throughout history when people have prayed they are connecting to the highest level and best place known to them, and so the prayers being said tend to just fill up the place and fill the room with spirit. The repetitive nature of those prayers calls

upon, and draws upon, a river of magnificence of all those who have said these prayers before. So you are inviting that river into the place, into this room where the person is passing over, helping them to let go, to move into their higher place.

Made-up prayers do not hold the potency; you must use prayers of a tradition which can either be said or played quietly in the background, as it invokes something higher than the self. It is easy to go into a mental understanding of these things, what our world looks like, what we've been conditioned to believe in, what we can prove scientifically—but science can't prove the spirit world.

When someone you love very dearly is at the moment of passing over, they are no longer in that world of understanding, so mental concepts are of no help to them. The spirit world is where they have stepped into, so if you have the privilege of stepping into the spirit world with them, to ensure that they are in a good place there, then spiritual practice of prayer or meditation is what you need to do. When they step into the spirit world it is a process that can go either quickly or slowly depending on the person. In essence what happens is the soul starts to leave the body and moves up through the energy points in the body until finally it comes out the top of the head and joins with the spirit.

So it's a bit like if you were to touch the feet or the knees of the person passing over, you can already feel the life force is gone from there. That will continue moving up the body, and is almost like lifting off a jumper until it is completely gone. Then the soul connects with the spirit, and the spirit moves up to its own highest place and in the process of this happening, again prayers keep the river flowing, helping them move up to all the levels they need to go to.

As the person breathes their last breath, visualise the energy or soul presence of the body travelling up through the spinal column, releasing at the top of the head at the crown chakra. When the person has died, visualise three golden steps and see yourself walking the steps with them and encouraging them to go through the door where all of their loved ones have been waiting for them.

It is a myth to believe that our grief holds their spirit here, but rather our grief and sadness are felt by our loved ones as overwhelming love and this facilitates them in their onward journey. Prayers of any faith tradition are important for the deceased relative or friend for up to a month or more afterwards.

We need to be aware that when we are on earth we only have about a tenth of who we really are, and so when the person is passing over they are now returning to the other ninety percent, the absolute fullness of all that they are. Not only are they connecting now to that hundred percent but they are also connecting with a hundred percent of all the ancestors and those whom they have loved before. The nicest thing of all is that if you are helping them pass over, you who are only ten percent here on earth, the person passing over can now connect with your higher self, the other ninety percent of you that they may not have known or only maybe sensed from time to time but hadn't seen before. In their passing over they reach a tremendous place of fulfilment with the fullness and richness of everyone they have ever known being with them.

This is when death is a natural occurrence, when it is time for the person to go. Nobody knows that except the person's higher self, their spirit and Source. Spirit has decided with the higher self of that person when it is their time to go. So the process described is what happens only in a natural death and does not apply to death by suicide which is different.

So for example when a parent loses a child a whole aspect of the parent (or both parents) goes with the child and a new aspect of the parent comes into being. So the child does not feel separation from the parent at all. And this is why people often notice a huge change in the person when they have lost a child, it is because a new aspect of the parent has come in. The comforting thing about this is that the child who has passed over is safely with a parent or both parents. Sometimes it's the mother, sometimes it's the father. Often if there are other children, it is one parent who goes and the other parent remains so that parent maintains the continuity within the family. It doesn't affect how much love there is within the family or how much love there would be for others but there is a difference in the parent's character in the aftermath.

When somebody is passing over and may be in pain, in a great deal of pain, and they are somebody you love very much, you just wish they were out of this pain. Here is the hardest thing of all—you have to accept that this person is doing something on behalf of the family line, they are often releasing a great sorrow or pain that either they have carried or that is in the genetic line. We must allow them to work through this process and make the journey through pain be about them and not us. Soon that process will be over and a bit like labour pains in childbirth, it is shockingly difficult pain to go through and to witness, but when labour is over and the baby is born there is joy. So the same for the person passing over, if they can, in carrying some of this pain, move some great sorrow or blocks through themselves they will break through to the other side and they will be so glad of what they have achieved.[12]

So the image is like running a big marathon, their feet are bleeding, they can hardly breathe, they are

12 Author's note: This is not to deny a person pain relief. We do everything we can in palliative care to alleviate symptoms, but not all pain can be medicated. Some of the angst of dying is part of all that must be processed on the individual journey and may be the cause of their suffering to which we must stay steadfastly present with prayer and meditation.

deeply emotional but very soon they are going to reach the finish line. If you come in just before the finish line and try to take them away, they will not thank you for this. They have lived their whole life, a full life, and this last push towards the end requires that we give them the privilege to do that. We must do all we can, but we do not have permission to take that work away from them. And if you pray or meditate on this you will find the answer every time, trust, trust Spirit will help them make it through to the other side. We have to trust that there is a spiritual midwife who is working with them from the other side, being present, helping them transition through the pain that at some level they have agreed to carry.

Their mind doesn't want the pain, their body doesn't want the pain, but their spirit is the one who will carry all the rewards. When you pass over the only thing you have is what you have achieved in this lifetime and so if you go through to the other side, releasing pain or trauma from the family line, it is like getting a huge reward for doing this work. As soon as they pass over the pain is gone just like childbirth—once birthed there is huge relief followed by joy. So as difficult as it is to watch, try to be like a midwife helping to birth this person over to the other side. It's about them, their journey. It is not about you, whoever you are—care provider, loved one—it is only about the person passing over. Try to remain present to the pain, aware that the pain is bringing them where they need to go. Again this is about them, not about you; love them enough to allow them to finish the journey they chose. It's not about taking them out of their pain but loving them by staying present with them as they near the finish line.

The reality is we live on a planet of sorrows and joys, with all life ending in death and that is so painful to so many. But it is better to acknowledge the pain that's here and to allow the person to work through, learning and gaining all they possibly can, carrying this through their soul and their spirit into the everlasting forever.

When a person has passed over it's important to understand that in all of the major traditions it is known that there are many places or levels a person can go. For example in Christian tradition, 'In my Father's house are many mansions',[13] and in Buddhist tradition there are many Bardo states. They are neither good or bad places necessarily, but each person is brought to the place most suitable to them, a place most familiar, most comfortable to them. And from that place as they are able and ready, people who have loved them, and their own spirit guides, will show them their life. They will be shown all the positives of their lives and also the things they could have done differently. They have to look at and face everything, accepting where they are and who they are. A hundred percent of

---

13 Bible, King James Version, John 14:2.

who you are is revealed to you, how a small kindness could have elevated you to many, many levels in the afterlife existence. And how an anger or a slight could have held you back from a wonderful opportunity and you get to see this within yourself. You then get a chance to work on those areas, if you wish.

If the soul doesn't pass over to spirit, for example in a sudden death, he/she may be concerned for the family and want to stay on the earth to help them in some way. There is a problem with this, it being that if this person doesn't go back to their highest place, he or she has no power and cannot help their husband or wife and family. Even though this was an accident, if it wasn't the person's time it simply would not have happened. If the person is not in their right place, their family will be left with an unease, a feeling that something is wrong, a feeling that can delay the natural bereavement process. The feeling can sometimes be so strong and uncomfortable for a loved one, it is as though he or she is now what we imagine as a ghost. He or she is very lost, for they are neither in the physical world or in the spirit world; they are not in their right place. This is why it is imperative that the right prayers and help be given to the person from a spiritual source. Ceremony and ritual are needed to facilitate the soul passing over to their right place. The ceremony and ritual need to be done with deep reverence, awareness and spiritual power by people of strong faith belief of any tradition, whether Priest, Buddhist Lama, Imam or Healer. It is very valuable to have prayers or chanting done in one's own tradition so that the person who has passed over will feel and benefit from these prayers in their immediate transition to spirit. We owe it to our loved ones to invest spiritually in their wellbeing. The ceremony is of particular importance in an unanticipated and sudden death and in particular following death by suicide.

When someone we love is dying or has just passed over, the biggest challenge for all of us remains to not make it about us but about the loved one in that moment. The sensitivity, the continued awareness that's needed in those moments when the person has stopped breathing is all too often overlooked, as it is likely to prompt a collapse into our own grief. To just give the person time, to put our own emotions on hold in those immediate few minutes after death is so important. It may require just leaving the bedside or the room if it becomes too much and you feel the need to release. While we are sitting with a dying loved one, we need to remind ourselves that we are in a very privileged place whereby the spirit world is working with us and sensitivity to noise and energy in the room is most important to the onward departure of our loved one.

To remain in a place of pure love, to keep silent prayer or meditation in those moments is important for our loved one in facilitating their passing over.

After a time has passed, grief should be allowed to flow gently and easily, feeling the release and being bathed by the energy of love, remembering that all of our grief is eventually felt by our loved ones in spirit as love. Allow the feeling of peace to wash over you while being with them in that space between, having been yourself touched by Spirit.

9

Onward Journey

THE LATE SEAMUS HEANEY, much-loved Irish poet and Nobel Laureate, described the scene at his mother's deathbed at the moment of her final passing, 'The space we stood around was emptied into us to keep'.[14] He likens death to the physical falling of a tree and that in the aftermath, a clearing comes.

And so with loss, an empty space is felt when our loved one dies. In these heartfelt empty spaces we remind ourselves that the love shared never dies, but is our lifelong gift to keep. The treasure trove of memories emptied into us can be used as a healing elixir for our broken hearts, as we grieve our loved ones' physical absence in the world.

There is another world that lies beside us all the time, a world we rarely contemplate until someone we love dies, and that is the invisible world of spirit. Our loved ones go on to that other world we cannot see with outward eyes, leaving us lonely as we feel and sense their physical absence in our day-to-day lives. Finding time to gently close our eyes, quiet our minds and open the door of

---

14 Heaney, S. *The Haw Lantern.*

our hearts, there, in the quiet stillness of our being, we can sense again our loved ones, close to us in spirit.

Reflecting on thirty years of work in healthcare at the threshold of birth and death, I am heartened by the compassion of those wholeheartedly present and authentically caring for people either entering or taking their leave of the physical world. I trust and feel the support that is there on the other side of the doorsill where the two worlds meet, as those in spirit whom we have loved and who have gone before us reach out and touch the caregivers in the handover of their loved one to Spirit. It is a reminder of why so much is felt by those present in such tender moments of transition, and in the aftermath.

As we evolve and grow through all the life lessons we are given to experience in the physical world, it is the dance between light and darkness, joy and sorrow, love and loss, that gifts new depth and meaning to the intricate tapestry of our lives. Being at the threshold of birth and death, we each become the holders of hope in understanding one of life's essential truths, that light always follows darkness.

In concluding our journey together reflecting on love and loss, I offer the following dedication to all those journeying between worlds.

May you be bathed in love and healing light
In your new form, may you continue to mind and
guide those who loved you
And who brought you into being, allowing you to
fulfil your individual destiny
May light flood from your etheric heart to all those
who held and loved you
And may all who grieve your loss feel your love in
quiet moments of their lives,
In both heart and spirit.

Acknowledgements

This book could not have come into being without the following individuals who invested so much of their time and energy, generously. It took a large team of spiritual midwives, who arrived at different stages of the book's gestation and labour, to help me birth it. I also wish to acknowledge those in my life without whose support and encouragement I might not have set out on this journey.

In old Celtic times it was thought that to travel to Skellig Michael and climb this 'perilous rock' off the west coast of Kerry, was to undertake a pilgrimage of sorts. And people of that time believed that in undertaking this pilgrimage, it would be of benefit to them when it was their time to die. That is my wish, for those who came at different junctures to work on the book, may each one of you remember this shared pilgrimage and be blessed when your time comes to journey to that other world.

To Maria Rawlins, for prompting me to write, for coaxing me, for encouraging me and finally, for almost killing me in the process! Like all good midwives she reminded me throughout the long labour and solitary process that 'the baby' would one day emerge, and I'd forget all the hard work of bringing it into being. For her wisdom, her spiritual guidance and for sharing her unique insights on birth and death, two pivotal pieces of the book.

To Catherine de Courcy a visionary writer whose practical no nonsense approach moved the work on through all the different stages. Her steadfast support to me began in France some years ago and having walked step by step along the path she guided us all through to the finish line. Catherine's knowledge of writing and the publication process was invaluable. So too was her initial rapture of each human story and her intention to help bring this small book into the public domain.

To Maeve Ann Austen, whose timely arrival in the development of the book structure was imperative, as she set out on the onerous task of excavating the golden statue that lay hidden beneath much rubble. Maeve Ann's gentle nature and warm loving energy helped me in ways I can't articulate. She befriended me in my grief of letting so much go, and I am eternally grateful for all the time and heart she invested in this book.

To Anne Dodd, whom I trust implicitly with all things close to my heart. Anne was the first person I entrusted 'a massive big overgrown text' to, after a year of initial writing. She helped identify all the threads that were emerging, as we giggled and laughed at the kitchen table, helping to allay all the anxiety I held in sharing my stories for the first time. I was and remain, deeply grateful for her support in setting out on this long road.

To Ann Cameron, who arrived as the copy editor but exceeded all expectations. Her work on this book has been immense. Ann's spiritual insight, her love and deep engagement with all those written about added a whole new dimension to book editing. She brought grace and light to the process, affording me warmth and reassurance all the way. Ann worked quietly away for months like an alchemist, distilling the pages into a healing elixir for our collective hearts. I am grateful to the spirit world for placing Ann in the right place at the right time for all the right reasons.

To the proof readers, Aileen Fennessy and Marleen Duffy, who offered insightful feedback. They came to the book edits without my knowing that each had a baby sibling in spirit; Baby Robert and Baby Michael. To Kirsten DeLeo for her review and feedback of the draft manuscript. To Frank, Margaret and Liz for their heroic efforts in the final hours.

To Sarah and Terry Fahey, for allowing me to share their Tom's precious story with the world.

To all the artists, most notably Siobhan McDonald for the investment of her time, energy and aesthetic input. To Yvette Monaghan for a healing connection through the camera lens. To Maria Callaghan, my very own artistic director for the last twenty years.

To Karen Carty of Anú Design for her creative talents and professional service. And to her team, in particular Terry, for his expertise in cover design and graphics.

To all those in the spirit world about whom I wrote, some named, some anonymised. Thank you for staying with me throughout this long and sometimes lonely road. For your help in bringing the right people in and out at different stages, for reminding me always of its higher purpose and for signalling clearly to me the right timing of its birth. In bringing this small book to print I entrust it's potential healing power to you, to guide and direct its path into people's hearts.

To all the wisdom teachers whose workshops, writings and philosophies fuelled my own spiritual quest and search for truth. To the spiritual care team at Dzogchen Beara, the Kryia Yoga Sanga in Ireland and Vienna, and my mindfulness regional group who remain soulful friends.

To all the healers in my world, an endless list. Special thanks to my Reiki teachers, both past and present, who opened my heart and mind to broader understandings of life, for holding me through my own life losses and challenges, and teaching me beyond words.

To my Mother and Father who brought me into being. My Mother, for her vivacious character, her love of the dying and for introducing me to all the finer things in life. My Father for his quiet gentle demeanour, his prayerful life and deep connection to the land and nature.

To my three brothers, Sean, Frank and Niall who bring me back to my roots regularly and keep me grounded. To my three sisters-in-law, who birthed beautiful little souls into the world, all my nieces and nephews whom I love and who adorn my life with so much joy.

To my circle of very close friends who have known the intricate tapestry of my life for years, as well as a treasured group of 'Wisdom Women' at the Coombe hospital, old friends in public health nursing in particular those who mentored and guided me, friends from the 'Sacred Grace' meetings and the three powerful women I met during my Masters program at the Irish Hospice Foundation who became lifelong friends. I am deeply grateful for both your individual and collective wise counsel and timeless friendship. May we continue to love, laugh and cry through all the joys and sorrows of life.

To a small group of friends I came to know as the men's group, the Irish team who set up the charity *New Growth*, supporting sustainable living with farmers in Nepal. May the fruits of your labour continue for generations to come long after you have left this world. Special thanks to Neil McCann for carefully reviewing this manuscript with his legal eye and healing heart.

To Kim Adzich who came late to the process but whose arrival into my life was akin to that first cup of tea mothers enjoy after giving birth; like nothing ever tasted before, sublime. To his credit, he managed to turn my quiet meditative life on its head in the most positive of ways. For coming to live in Ireland and for embarking with me on a great big adventure, opening doors for a whole new life chapter in British Columbia, Canada. For his shared passion in care of the dying, his endless support, and above all else, his love.

To my colleagues in healthcare, may you be reminded constantly of your good hearts. May the love and compassion you bestow on others come back to you multiplied in your own life's journey. May you be met with kindness when your time comes to die.

To all the patients and families I was honoured to meet and journey with. To those who invited me into their inner world and allowed me to hold their hearts for a period of time, I am eternally grateful. In all the busy healthcare worlds I have inhabited over a thirty year span, time and time again when organisational stresses arose my sanctuary always fell to human contact. Patients have been my refuge for years, and they remain so today.

Finally I wish to conclude by acknowledging that I now live on the traditional and unceded territory of the Coast Salish Peoples, the traditional territory of the Quw'utsun (Cowichan) Tribes. In doing so I bow to both the ancestors and elders of this community and humbly seek their blessing to continue my healing work in this land.

About the Author

Bríd Shine is a Registered Nurse and Registered Midwife accredited with the Nursing & Midwifery Board of Ireland. She holds a Higher Diploma in Public Health Studies from University College Dublin and a Master's Degree in Bereavement Studies from the Royal College of Surgeons Ireland. With over thirty years' experience, she has cared for individuals and their families in both the hospital and community setting at all stages of the life cycle from birth to death and beyond.

Bríd's most recent role within healthcare was a decade of work in the area of Perinatal Palliative Care and Bereavement. During this time she also worked at a national level in the development of National Bereavement Standards for Ireland's maternity hospitals. Bríd has a close affiliation with the Irish Hospice Foundation, whose dome-shaped library became the womb space that facilitated her studies during her Master's Degree. Here too she undertook training in the area of Complicated Grief with Dr Kathy Shear and facilitated workshops on perinatal bereavement care.

Bríd is a certified teacher of Mindfulness-Based Stress Reduction (MBSR), training with the Institute for Mindfulness-Based Approaches (IMA) in Europe. She facilitates workshops on meditation and self-compassion for healthcare professionals. Bríd has also undertaken professional training in Ireland and Denmark, including 'Mindfulness in Medicine' with the founder of MBSR, Dr Jon Kabat Zinn of the Centre of Mindfulness, University of Massachusetts.

Bríd's growing interest in the area of mind-body medicine resulted from training in both Ireland and the U.S. with Dr Deepak Chopra and the late Dr David Simon of the Chopra Center, California. Bríd is a certified Reiki healing practitioner and has also been certified with the Pure Energy Healing Academy in Spain.

In 2007, having undertaken a ten-day retreat with Buddhist teacher and author of *The Tibetan Book of Living & Dying*, Bríd began a series of accredited trainings with the spiritual care programme at Dzogchen Beara, a Buddhist retreat centre perched on a cliff overlooking the Atlantic Ocean on the southwest coast of Ireland. This included programmes in spiritual care of the dying, deep active listening courses and meditation workshops. In 2009, she attended Ireland's first international Spiritual Care of the Dying conference, *Compassion and Presence,* organised by the Dzogchen Beara spiritual care team, with renowned leaders in the area of holistic palliative care. More recently in 2019 she undertook their Contemplative End of Life Care training programme, *Authentic Presence.* Bríd considers Dzogchen Beara her spiritual home and returns frequently for alone time to maintain her own wellbeing when working in a busy clinical environment.

While the teachings of Tibetan Buddhism were to spark and ignite in Bríd her professional desire to work with the dying, this desire harboured within her soul and psyche was ever-present from her early childhood as she witnessed first-hand her own mother's love and compassion in caring for the dying. It is therefore to this teacher, her late mother Margaret Shine (née Nolan), that this book is lovingly dedicated.

Bibliography

Brach, Tara. *Radical Acceptance*. New York, NY: Random House, 2000.

Byock, Ira. Dying Well. New York, NY: Riverhead Books, 1998.

Groves, Richard F., and Klauser, Henrietta Anne. *The American Book of Living and Dying: Lessons in Healing Spiritual Pain*. United States, Celestial Arts, 2009.

Heaney, Seamus. *The Haw Lantern*. London: Faber and Faber, 1987.

Kabat-Zinn, Jon. *Coming to our Senses*. London, UK: Little, Brown Book Group, 2005.

Kabat-Zinn, Jon. *Wherever You Go, There You Are*. London, UK: Little, Brown Book Group, 2005.

Klass, Dennis, et al. *Continuing Bonds: New Understandings of Grief*. Abingdon, UK: Taylor & Francis, 1996.

Kubler-Ross, Elisabeth. *On Death & Dying*. New York, NY: Macmillan Publishing, 1969.

Lesser, Elizabeth. *Broken Open: How Difficult Times Can Help Us Grow*. New York, NY: Random House Books, Inc., 2004.

Lewis, C. S. *A Grief Observed*. New York, NY: HarperCollins Publishers, 1994.

Longaker, Christine. *Facing Death & Finding Hope*. New York, NY: Doubleday, 1997.

Neimeyer, Robert. *Meaning Reconstruction and the Experience of Loss*. Washington, D.C.: American Psychological Association, 2001.

O'Donohue, John. *Anam Cara: Spiritual Wisdom from the Celtic*

World. New York, NY: Harper Collins Publishers, 1997.

O'Donohue, John. *Benedictus: A Book of Blessings*. New York, NY: Bantam Books, 2012.

O'Donohue, John. *Divine Beauty: The Invisible Embrace*. London, UK: Transworld Publishers Ltd, 2004.

O'Donohue, John. *Eternal Echoes*. New York, NY: HarperCollins Publishers, 1999.

O'Donohue, John. *To Bless the Space Between Us*. New York: Doubleday, 2008.

Papadatou, Danai. *In the Face of Death: Professionals Who Care for the Dying and the Bereaved*. New York, NY: Springer Publishing Company, 2009.

Rogers, Carl. *On Becoming a Person*. London, UK: Little, Brown Book Group, 2003.

Rumi. *The Essential Rumi*. Translated by Coleman Barks. New York: Harper Collins Publishers, 1995.

Santorelli, Saki. *Heal Thy Self*. New York, NY: Random House, 2000.

Saunders, Cicely. *Living with the Dying: Management of Terminal Disease*. Oxford, UK: Oxford University Press, 1989.

Sogyal Rinpoche. *The Tibetan Book of Living and Dying*. 2nd Ed. San Francisco: Harper Collins, 2002.

Thich Nhat Hanh. *No Death, No Fear: Comforting Wisdom for Life*. New York: Riverhead Books, 2002.

Tobin, Daniel R. *Peaceful Dying*. Boston: Da Capo Press, 1968.

Yeats, W.B. *'The Stolen Child'. The Collected Works of W. B. Yeats*. London: Collectors Library, 2010.

Printed in Germany
by Amazon Distribution
GmbH, Leipzig

23384107R00082